Lovely Love

All you need to know to make your love happy

Luang Phaw Dhammajayo

Published by
Foundation of Wisdom Perfection
Mr. Somchai Laopeamthong
88/136 Mu 4, Charoensuk 4 Village
Soi Senanikom 1, Paholyotin Road
Chorakaebua Sub-District
Ladprao District, Bangkok
Thailand 10230
Tel: (66+2) 553-0496, (66+8) 1494-9072

Edited, Designed, and Distributed by
The Print Lodge Pte Ltd
16 Arumugam Road
#03-04 Lion Building D
Singapore 409961
info@theprintlodge.com.sg
Tel: (65) 6746 6520

ISBN: 978-981-08-0044-4 (Singapore)

Printed in Thailand by Rung Silp Printing

Contents

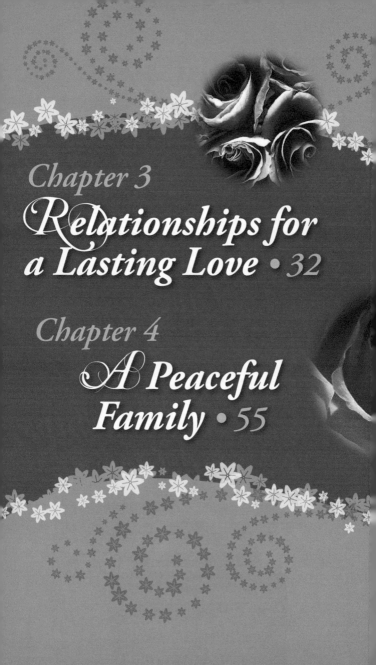

Introduction

Love has existed for a long time because mankind has love in their hearts throughout their lifetime on Earth. Love is innate in us ever since we are born. As an infant, we were brought up by our parents who gave us warmth and tenderness. We were also surrounded by relatives who adore us. As we grow up, beloved friends come into our lives – boys, girls, men and women of various ages coming from all walks of life. Over time, love extends its branches to become couple love, which further blooms into marriage. Through this union, we bear our offspring. Taking care of our children is a responsibility in life that we have to carry out with love. As time passes and as we get older, we impart wisdom gained through our life experiences and shower bountiful love to our younger generation.

Many people spend their lives giving love to others and receiving love from others. For innumerable times, they often encounter both satisfaction and disappointment. Even when death is near and it is time for them to depart, some people still struggle with love that is not reciprocated. Sadly, they leave the world without a good understanding of love.

This book *Lovely Love* will give you precious insight about love in different aspects. It will also serve as a guide that will help to develop one's love to be more beautiful and complete, whether it is love towards one's girlfriend, boyfriend, spouse, parents, siblings or oneself. Amongst all kinds of love, the only superior love that supersedes all others is universal love. Everyone should learn how to attain universal love – it is a love which is pure, all encompassing, complete and powerful. This type of love can easily be attained through meditation practice.

This book also includes testimonies from people who are blessed by endless love in their lives, all made possible through meditation and *Dhamma* practice. In the book, you will discover that the study and practice of *Dhamma* can help you to improve your love life. You will love others as well as yourself in the right way, bringing about a happy and enriching life. Most importantly, universal love will blossom within you, and you will soon be ready to bring great positive changes to your life and to others around you.

Heavenly Home

For members of a family
Who share love and sympathy with one another
Father and mother showing great care
The home is heavenly sweet
Understanding and knowing
Bringing about great warmth
It will be cold
Even if you bathe under the summer sunshine
If everyone at home loses their ties
Living by oneself ... never joining to help
Even forgetting to encourage
Happiness and joy start from the mind
The pure minds of those who belong
Having pure minds and becoming one
Very soon, the dream will be real

Luang Phaw Dhammajayo

Chapter 1 *Love*

Connection from Past Existence

The love between two people, whether it is love at first sight, or love that slowly blossoms, has a lot to do with their relationships in previous lives. The Lord Buddha explained that love develops from two main causes: the couple may have been husband and wife in previous lives; or have cared for each other in the present life.

Take the case of Prince Siddhattha (the Buddha himself, before renouncing the world and entered ordination) and his wife, Princess Bimba. They had pursued *Perfections* (supreme virtues to be performed by one who wishes to attain enlightenment otherwise known as *parami*) together throughout many past lifetimes. In one lifetime, Siddhattha was born as an ascetic named Sumedha, a *Bodhisatta* (one who is destined to be a Buddha) who dedicated himself in the pursuit of *Perfections*.

Once upon a time, a Buddha of that epoch named Dipankara and his disciples were passing through a city and approached a large puddle of water in their path. In a virtuous act, Sumedha laid his body across the puddle to let Dipankara Buddha and his disciples walk over to the other side, so they would not get wet. Dipankara Buddha prophesied that Sumedha would become the next Buddha, known as Gotama.

Bimba was a village woman in that lifetime. She and Sumedha did not know each other. Upon seeing Sumedha's admirable act, she became fond of him and fell in love. She made an earnest wish to become Sumedha's wife, and to be reborn as his wife in every future lifetime.

From that lifetime onwards, whenever Princess Bimba was reborn, she would become his life partner, and would pursue *Perfections* together until their final lifetime, where they separately attained *Nibbana* (known as nirvana in *sanskrit*) and were no longer subjected to rebirth.

Love and bond grounded on virtues bind a couple together through many lifetimes. Their past connection leads them to fall in love and care for each other. Some couples feel an instant connection, because they have made earnest wishes from a previous existence to meet again in future lives. This explains why

some people fall in love at first sight.

Although a connection from previous existences may exist for many couples, it does not mean that their love will necessarily be smooth and happy.

When people are young and fall in love for the first time, they tend to be sweet and affectionate to each other. Some would even make resolutions or vows promising to love each other and live together forever. These are the kinds of wishes that are often made by people who are experiencing a new love.

Once they have been together long enough, their passion for each other may gradually diminish and they soon stop making efforts to please each other. As people get older, they naturally become less attractive, and may even seem to appear 'boring' to each other. When a husband or wife looks for a way out, or gets attracted by someone who is more appealing, this is when all the problems turn into chaos and start to wreck a marriage.

Living together with another person is likened to wearing bracelets; a single bracelet makes no noise, but when two bracelets are worn together, they rattle and jangle.

Actions in the present lifetime also matter a great deal. Couples who are true friends and encourage good things for each other tend to be happier and stay together longer. As for those couples who have not performed many merits together, their love for each other will dissipate over time. They will end up separating from each other through divorce or death.

The length of time a couple might live together is determined by the merits they have accrued together in previous lifetimes, by whether they have been lovers in their past existences and also by how supportive they were of each other in their present lifetime. Like a lotus that relies on the combination of water and earth to grow, success of the love between two people depends heavily on the above-mentioned factors.

Inner Qualities

Although relationships from a previous lifetime may be a catalyst for current love, we still need to be prudent and apply wise principles when selecting the right life partner. Love alone is not sufficient to determine whether a person will be one's best life partner.

In choosing a life partner, we should look for someone who shares the same views as ourselves, and who has mutual respect for each other. Since this person will likely be the parent to our children, he or she has to be a good role model for them. We should not base our decision mainly on physical appearance, wealth and personal abilities.

Physical attraction is short-lived. We should determine whether our life partner has similar virtues as ourselves, that is, similar faith, morality and views. Do they have a strong faith in *The Triple Gem* (triple refuge consisting of Buddha, *Dhamma* and *Sangha*) as we do? Do they observe *The Five Precepts* (codes of moral conduct)? Do they possess *The Right View* (right understanding of the Truth)? Do they believe in the *Law of Kamma* (law of cause and effect), etc? If these virtuous qualities

are shared, there is a better chance of building a long-lasting marriage.

In the beginning of a relationship, we are often contrived to make ourselves attractive. Sometimes, we do things beyond our normal behaviour in order to attract the other person to fall in love with us. Unfortunately, this strategy will not lead to a happy union. We have to take the time to learn about the other person's true self, just as he or she ought to learn about ours. Once a foundation of mutual understanding, mutual respect and shared virtues is built, a happy marriage will follow.

Marriage - a Dhamma point of view

Marriage forms an integral part of our lives. Thus, before we enter this union, we need to analyse carefully the reason why we marry. If we cannot find a good reason, it means that we are probably not ready to marry. Love alone is not reliable, because it is likely we may change our minds later. There should be something greater, something that makes a marriage worthwhile, a binding of two lives.

Whoever wants to enter a marriage should contemplate carefully. Indeed, the purpose of marriage is to be a true friend to one another, to look out for each other, and to be a partner in the pursuit of *Perfections*. Ideally, a married couple should share an equal faith in *The Triple Gem, The Five Precepts, The Right View* and *The Law of Kamma*.

In life, we will encounter many obstacles, stress and problems because our world is governed by what is known as *The Eight Worldly*

Conditions (*Lokadhamma*), which states that "nothing is constant, everything is subjected to change". These conditions comprise gain and loss, dignity and obscurity, praise and blame, as well as happiness and pain.

Our attachment to worldly matters always results in suffering. As a result, our efforts in the pursuit of *Perfections* can run into obstacles and we can lose sight of the ultimate goal of achieving *Nibbana*. A good soulmate can play an important role in steering us back onto the right path, the path of *Dhamma*. If our partner falters in his or her pursuit of *Perfections*, it should also be our responsibility to help the person get back on the path.

Chapter 2
Relationships and Love

People spend a fortune on research, books and other sources of information trying to discover the 'secret' to a successful and lasting marriage. Yet, every year, statistics show a grim reality that divorces are on the increase. Studies also show that children who grow up in broken homes tend to have more problems at school and in their emotional development compared to other kids.

Thus, it is fair to say that problems in a marriage can lead to problems in society. Many authors, doctors and self-help gurus offer their advice and remedy on the topic, but their proposed solutions come from the same people who are themselves imperfect because they are still subject to defilements such as greed, anger and delusion.

The Lord Buddha has given us invaluable *Dhamma* teachings on how to maintain a healthy marriage and how to be effective parents. These teachings have been preserved for over 2,500 years and it would be beneficial to us if we learn about them.

Delicate Love

Buddhist traditions serve as wonderful guidelines for a couple's married life. If we are to study Buddhist traditions, we will learn to distinguish which actions are appropriate and inappropriate, as well as how to restrain from carrying out inappropriate actions. This knowledge covers every aspect of a person's life, including how to build relationships that are ethical and conform to *The Five Precepts*.

Our Buddhist ancestors' view of love was nobler than what we find in modern times. In examining their ways, we learn how they valued their families for joining them in the pursuit of *Perfections* and for their roles in being the mother or father to their children. They did not condone promiscuity and sexual intimacy before marriage.

If we can reaffirm this sound Buddhist tradition and have the strength to prevail over our desires, we will become proud of ourselves, and be praised and honoured by all. Our behaviour will act as moral standards for our family as well as future generations. Children born into our family will be proud of this legacy.

Short-Term Pleasure

It is normal for a married couple to engage in sexual intimacy as long as they adhere to morality, decency and the law. Nevertheless, we should not become obsessed with it. Over-indulgence in intimacy could result in having unhealthy emotions such as jealousy, possessiveness, suspicion and fear of betrayal. We should not engage in intimacy with a lack of awareness or self-worth. Short-term pleasure sometimes results in long-term consequences.

Intimacy should only be shared between a married couple, not before they are married. Extra-marital affairs are inappropriate, and will lead to negative karmic consequences in *Samsara*, the cycle of existence. Buddhism considers sexual relations between partners as

something that is to be dignified, not indulged. Adultery is a violation of the fundamental Buddhist code of moral conduct.

Love is noble. Love is also the force that allows a man and a woman to pick out each other, from the crowd of seven billion people, to become one another's life partner. True companions should encourage each other to perform good deeds and to accumulate merits so they can both reach the goal of *Nibbana*. This sacred union also serves as the path for the birth of virtuous people into this world to pursue *Perfections*.

Since we exist in a world dominated by sensual pleasures, it is essential for us to realise that entering relationships simply as a diversion is not a good idea. If we are to bring another worthy human being into this world, it should be accomplished with pride and dignity.

You may have heard that love and desire go together. But love must come before desire. Love brings husband and wife together so that they may procreate and usher a human life into this world. Thus, they transform their roles as husband and wife to that of a father and mother.

Fathers and mothers are regarded as the noble ones of the household. The titles 'father' and 'mother' are honourable titles. However, many people today tend to overlook the importance of marriage. They allow only desire to dictate their decisions and actions. Unfortunately, this lack of discipline creates many ill consequences.

Lovely Love

Love depreciates in value when it is tarnished by sexual obsession and promiscuity. Promiscuity begins with roaming around, drinking, womanising, using drugs and gambling. Some students living far away from their parents for the first time suddenly find themselves becoming more independent and free. They start spending late nights with their friends and experimenting with sex, thinking that it is trendy, cool, stylish and acceptable. But what they fail to realise is that their behaviour accumulate negative karmic consequences and retribution which they have to pay later.

To avert this type of behaviour, parents must teach their children self-discipline, not only of the body but also of the mind. Teach them to respect the *Dhamma* and *The Law of Kamma*, so that they know the truth about life and existence. Then, they will understand the ill consequences that can take effect in this lifetime and the next, as well as the deterioration of the body and mind that can take place through careless acts.

Things that are precious to us must be preserved until the time is right. This is something that we have to remind ourselves at all times, otherwise it may reduce our sense of self-worth. Human life can only occur with a man and a woman, but should only be when it is appropriate. Promiscuity, illicit affairs and sexual violations lead to broken marriages, deceit and abortions, which in turn have their own karmic consequences.

Young people tend to focus on sex without realising the full consequences of their actions. In addition to loss of reputation or the dangers of sexually-transmitted diseases, there is always the possibility of an unexpected pregnancy. Many young couples who find themselves in this situation turn to abortion to solve their problem. They do not want the burden of raising a child when they are ill-prepared.

This solution may benefit them initially but if one looks at it from the spiritual perspective, the action is not justified at all. In fact, they have doomed themselves to many lifetimes of misfortune. After they die, they will have to suffer the consequences in the unhappy realms for many lifetimes. When they can be reborn as human beings again, they will be born into the womb of a mother who will also seek abortion as her solution. They will be prematurely terminated in many rebirths.

The Law of Kamma states that each individual is entitled to his own death when his time comes. It is no one's right to choose it for him. Whatever reasons one may find to seek abortion, whether it is the lack of financial security, poor health of a child or that the parents are too young and immature, we can never justify ending the life of another person.

Preserve and protect your most valued possession – yourself – and offer it only to the person whom you choose to spend your life and pursue *Perfections* with. We should never forget that if we choose to engage in sexual intimacy, it should always be done with love and regard for our partner. Although modern attitudes and the media promote an obsessive focus on sex and sensuality, the Lord Buddha taught us to always retain our wisdom and self-respect with matters of the heart. That is a timeless lesson we can all benefit.

Chapter 3
Relationships for a Lasting Love

Seven Types of Spouses

Before learning about the different ingredients for a lasting marriage, we need to know what type of husband or wife we are in order to embark on the appropriate improvements. The sermon about the seven types of spouses was presented by the Lord Buddha some 2,500 years ago, but His teachings remain relevant today. In His sermon, the Lord Buddha described the seven types of spouses:

1. A spouse like a murderer:

Such a spouse has no sympathy, compassion or gratitude towards the other, and is unfaithful. Marriage with such a partner is like living with an enemy.

2. A spouse like a thief:

Such a spouse has no sense of financial responsibility or accountability. This spouse is extravagant, irresponsible and may even run up debts for the family. Marriage with such a partner is like having a thief in the household.

3. A spouse like a boss:

Acting like a bullying boss, this spouse robs the dignity of the other. Marrying to such a spouse is like having a boss in the house, commanding whatever you do.

4. A spouse like a parent:

Such a spouse looks after the other with the same care as a parent would look after his or her own child. When the other spouse suffers a misfortune, or becomes sick or disabled, this spouse will stay faithful and look after the other spouse until his or her last breath.

5. A spouse like a sibling:

Such a spouse is truthful and loyal to the other. The love from this spouse is long-lasting.

6. A spouse like a friend:

This spouse is loyal and supportive, and will stand by the other spouse in good and bad times just like a true friend would.

7. A spouse like a servant:

Such a spouse is honest and loyal and would take abusive treatments without retaliation, but tends to behave like a servant to the other.

Living with the first three types of spouses is like living in hell. As a result of all the terrible things that the husband and wife have done to each other, the bad kamma they have created for themselves will almost certainly drive them into an unhappy realm after they pass away. It is bad luck to be married to the first three types of spouses.

Most husbands and wives have varying degrees of characteristics from each of the above-mentioned types. Obviously, some characteristics are more positive than others, but we must nevertheless strive to be a good husband or wife. Be a spouse like a parent, a friend and a sibling and be helpful towards each other.

Now that we know what types of husband or wife there are, let us find out the types of married couples that exist. The following are some examples:

Type 1 – Mr Yakkha (ogre) marrying Ms Yakkhini (ogress):

In the past, they might have loved each other at first sight, but now they 'fight at first sight'. They quarrel everyday, bringing out the worst of one another.

Type 2 – Mr Deva (angel) marrying Ms Yakkhini (ogress):

The husband is a 'prince charming', but the wife is an 'ugly toad' who is rude, crude and uncivil. The husband attends religious sessions at the temple while the wife is out gambling.

Type 3 – Ms Deva (angel) marrying Mr Yakkha (ogre):

Here, the wife is sweet and kind, but the husband is abusive and bad-tempered. The wife attends religious sessions at the temple while the husband is out drinking.

Lovely Love

Type 4 – Mr Deva (angel) marrying Ms Deva (angel):

The most compatible type of couple is one that consists of a Mr Deva and Ms Deva. They speak kindly to one another. They attend religious sessions at the temple together. They make charitable donations, observe *The Five Precepts*, practise meditation and support each other. They are a couple who accumulates merits and pursues *Perfections* together like a pair of angels living together on earth. Once we recognise which behaviour we and our spouse are exhibiting, we can make improvements and resolve to make our marriage more enjoyable. We can work together to solve potential problems that may arise in our marriage.

Continue working in our respective careers, make merit and meditate together as a couple. If we do not try to bring the best of ourselves into a marriage, we end up nurturing a dangerous wound in our relationship, and we will never find peace and harmony in our own home.

Advice for Sons-in-Law and Daughters-in-Law

Many people encounter a variety of problems in their marriages. For instance, a woman may not get along with her in-laws to the point that she and her husband can end up in divorce. For this kind of situation, perhaps we can learn from a story that took place during the time of the Buddha.

Once, there lived a woman named Visakha (a famous benefactor of the Buddha). She was the daughter of a millionaire named Dhananjaya. Visakha was to be married and would soon move from her parents' house to live with her future husband and his family. On the day that she moved out, Dhananjaya gave Visakha a ten-fold advice on how to be a good daughter-in-law. This 2,500 year-old advice is still practised and is applicable even up till today. It also applies to sons-in-law as well.

The points are as follows:

1. *Do not show our 'dirty laundry' in public.*

When we find faults in our in-laws, keep them to yourself. Keep the affairs of the family within the household. Do not go spreading the internal affairs of the family to outsiders.

2. Do not bring external problems or gossips into the house.

Should anyone speak about the faults of our in-laws, do not pass the gossips around.

3. Give to those who give to us.

Help those who return what we lend them. If we have helped, or lent money or things to people who returned them punctually, we should help or lend to these people again.

4. Do not give to those who do not give to us.

Do not lend money or things to people who refuse to return to us, even though it was within their capacity to do so.

5. Whether they give to us or not, give to them anyway.

Whether they have helped us in the past or not, if they are our relatives and have fallen on hard times, we should help them anyway.

Lovely Love

6. Sit with peace.

Know one's own position and behave according to the level of respect due to others. Be eager to help our in-laws. Welcome them well every time and do not turn away from them.

7. Eat with peace:

Provide food for our in-laws with special care. We may have to eat after the children. Once everyone is taken care of, when it is our time to eat, we will eat with peace.

8. Sleep with peace:

Make sure the work gets done before going to bed. Be the first to get up and the last to retire. When all the chores are taken care of, we will sleep with peace.

9. Preserve the fire:

'Fire', in this case, refers to the in-laws. They bring either trouble or happiness, so we need to keep an appropriate distance. This means that we have to deal with them carefully.

10. Respect the angels:

'Angels' in this case refer to the spouse's parents. We should treat them with respect at all times.

Although the style of the language used may sound old-fashioned, the meaning is still practical today. If we practise it, we will have a warm and loving home. It will make us more endearing and we are able to live together with our in-laws more harmoniously under one roof.

Lovely Love

Cool, Calm, Compromise, Complement and Smile!

Smiles are powerful weapons. It can disarm an angry person. Smiles are free; use them often. Smile at each other and we will see a decrease in tension. A husband or wife who knows how to smile at each other, how to stay calm and composed during an argument, how to compromise during a disagreement, and how to praise one another, will obtain a happy and lasting marriage. Smiles bring warmth and assurance to each other.

We need to continue to improve ourselves every day. If we want our spouse to understand and have faith in the power of merits, we should begin each day with a smile, and show our spouses how merits have indeed helped us become a better person. We should also know that we may not always be right all the time, and should not expect to have our way every time. Learn how to compromise.

Praise each other and treat our children with tenderness. Embrace our children often. Give them uplifting words, words of encouragement and praises. They will feel happy, motivated and inspired to keep doing the right things. But do not be excessive with our praises, or they may become frivolous.

A husband and wife should try to find good qualities in each other and speak positively among themselves. If our wife cooks a meal for us, give her compliments for her

effort. If there is something bothering us, keep calm and smile before we speak.

Pleasant speech is like honey. The words "I love you" are words of honey. The sweetness of these words can breathe life into our marriage and carry us from one lovely day to the next. It fulfils us like a good meal.

We cannot just eat a good meal every other year to be fulfilled; we need it as often as we can. Likewise, we need to feed our partner with the food of love frequently. We need to say it often and remind each other regularly of how much we love and care for each other. Even husbands and wives who have lived together for a long time need to regularly remind themselves of this fact. A wife may complain that her husband no longer tells her he loves her like he used to. He may make excuses that he has already said it 50 years ago, and that it still stands today. The truth is, the more "I love you" is said to the other party, the more there is love to be felt.

Love Simultaneously, Be Angry at Different Times

When a couple decides to live together, they must find ways to maintain their love. Since nobody is perfect, and since both individuals are normal human beings, each person has his or her own shortcomings. When we live alone, our shortcomings are kept to ourselves. But when we live with other people, our shortcomings become noticeable to others. We can deal with our own shortcomings

Lovely Love

but we will have less tolerance towards the shortcomings of others.

Living with other people brings out many issues and challenges that do not usually exist when we live by ourselves. What can two imperfect individuals do to maintain a peaceful household?

It is normal for married couples to disagree. When we disagree or get angry, try to keep our anger away from each other. We can be mad at each other, but avoid speaking angry words. Keep our anger away from each other. We may joke and say that we can take turns to get angry with each other – we are only allowed to get angry with our spouse in the morning, and our spouse can be angry with us in the afternoon. This may be a joke but there is truth in it. When one is angry but the other is in no mood to quarrel, then the anger is diffused. It takes two to tango. We cannot clap with one hand, so make sure we do not get mad at each other at the same time.

No matter how well two people have known each other or how long they have been together, one cannot assume that one's partner knows intuitively or exactly what the other partner needs or desires. The wise thing to do is to perform our duties for the family to the best of our ability at all times. The husband should strive to provide for his family, and the wife should make the home a warm, cozy and welcoming environment. Although there are many chores to carry out within a household, the priority of a spouse is to make his or her partner feel loved and comfortable in the home.

When a husband or wife goes to work, he or she may encounter many work-related problems and stress. On the way home, he or she may have to fight the traffic or get frustrated with things that are annoying and show up at home in a foul mood. This happens often. Occasionally, our spouse may feel the urge to unload his or her stress and frustrations on us by talking about the problems. Listen to each other without the need to offer advice or judgment, or taking on the other's problems to become our own.

As the saying goes, when a hot iron is plunged into cold water, the iron cools but the water heats. We do not want our own temperature to rise. Know when to say what. If our partner just needs a sympathetic ear, listen with sympathy and understanding. If our partner needs advice, give intelligent advice. If humour is needed to break the sadness, come up with a good joke.

So, use this approach: 'love simultaneously, be angry at different times' and we will obtain a more harmonious married life.

Superior Love through Superior Dhamma

Because we are human beings, none of us are perfect. We all come with a baggage of deficiencies. We can cope with our own deficiencies but we cannot tolerate someone else's. This is the human condition. Once we start living with another person, our own deficiencies and those of our partner's

Lovely Love

accumulate. How do we cope with the challenges that are part of a family life? We turn to the *Dhamma* for help.

In *Dhamma for Householders*, the Lord Buddha gave us valuable insights on how to deal with family issues. This *Dhamma* consists of four virtues: truthfulness, self-control, endurance and generosity. These are the four virtues that should be observed and practised if one wishes to live in this world with complete happiness and harmony. These virtues will allow the person to conduct his or her life morally and free from harm.

The Thai Buddhist forefathers have adopted a tradition that every man should be ordained as a monk at least once in his lifetime. This is such that he would have the opportunities to learn the *Dhamma*, to practise meditation, to be trained in discipline and to be a pure and refined individual.

This is truly a wonderful tradition. Women are encouraged to attend religious sessions at the temple regularly. Married women should listen to *Dhamma* sermons simultaneously with their ordained husbands, so that both will absorb knowledge and perform good deeds as a team. This knowledge will prepare them to be better spouses and better parents for their children.

Children form an important part of a marriage. We must know how to take care of our children, not just physically, but morally and spiritually as well. Also, it is our responsibility to provide our children with both worldly and spiritual knowledge.

Worldly knowledge enables our children to earn a living and survive in this world. Spiritual knowledge shows them how to be good human beings and survive in *samsara*, the endless cycle of existence.

Once we have provided our children with worldly education and spiritual knowledge through the *Dhamma*, and have conditioned them to do good deeds regularly, we can be sure that they will grow up to be wonderful adults who are capable of bringing pride and prosperity to the family.

Handling our love is like holding a little bird in our palm. It should be handled gently; not too loose or it will fly away, and not too tight or it will suffocate. Also, we should apply the practice of sharing, saying only kind words to one another, showing selflessness and maintaining the consistency of our relationship with our spouse.

Chapter 4
A Peaceful Family

Giver of Human Form

In order for a human being to be born, it requires the interaction between the father and mother. An astral body enters the father and stimulates a desire for contact and intimacy (via intercourse) with his wife. Once the intercourse takes place, the astral body then moves from the father into the womb of the mother. Once the child is born, the love and bond between mother and child solidifies.

Every human life starts this way. Everyone has a father and a mother and we must love them enormously because they are the ones who provide us with the genetic makeup for a human form.

The necessity to have the human form is immeasurable, because this is the only form that is able to perform and accumulate merit and to pursue *Perfections* until we attain *Nibbana*. Angels and Brahmas (higher spiritual beings) are beings that enjoy the fruits of their past wholesome deeds, while animals, hungry ghosts, demons and hell creatures are doomed to suffer in the unhappy realms and certainly cannot perform merit.

Our parents gave us the greatest gift of all – the human form. They endured the overwhelming task of raising us until we grow up. They provided us with education, advice, encouragement and gave us moral support when we are disheartened. It is through this human form that we are able to practise meditation, cultivate and purify our minds and to pursue *Perfections* in order to reach the ultimate goal of liberation through *Nibbana*. These virtues are beyond description. They deserve to have our unconditional love, loyalty and respect.

Attracting The Soul Prepared for Birth

The child that is going to be born to a father and a mother needs his or her own merits as well as those of the parents' as the driving force for its birth. If the parents have accumulated merit while making an earnest wish to conceive a worthy child, the power of their merits will attract a soul with equivalent merits to be born.

This is a kind of 'selective process' where likes attract. Worthy parents will be blessed with a worthy child and vice-versa. It is like a puzzle that fits perfectly with its adjoining pieces, arranged by merits.

When a child is born full of merits, he will be blessed with all the good qualities of fortunate existence. The strength of his merits will bring prosperity, admiration and good fortune to himself and his family.

However, if the child lacks merits, he brings with him numerous behavioural problems and causes calamities and misfortune to the parents. To add value to our own child's good merits, it is imperative for us to accumulate many merits ourselves and to set good examples for the child so he or she is accustomed to seeing and doing good deeds.

In order for our children to achieve meaningful goals in life, we must teach them well and be good role models for them. We can find invaluable lessons in the Lord Buddha's teachings. Learning these lessons before committing to a marriage will ensure that one is aware of the grounds for a happy, stable family. For that reason, the traditional Thai custom encourages young men to ordain and study the *Dhamma* and live the life of a disciplined and wholesome person.

Parents are their children's first and most influential teachers. Once the mother and father are educated in the teachings of the Buddha, they will be equipped to impart essential wisdom to their children. If they are unable to provide their children with the right kind of knowledge, their children will end up getting knowledge from other sources such as friends, television, the internet and books. Unfortunately, these sources do not always offer right information nor positive influences.

An important guidance that parents should give to their children pertains to love and lust. They must teach their children not to engage in sexual intimacy before marriage because it goes against Buddhist traditions and it jeopardises one's virtues.

Abstinence is not an outdated idea but is in fact a contemporary practice that exemplifies the nobleness in human behaviour. It is very important that we teach our children about abstinence without fear of offending them because it is our duty to look after their spiritual values. We need to educate them on the pros and cons as well as the benefits and dangers related to this subject, even if they call us old-fashioned and boring. We have to explain that intimacy before marriage should not be about being trendy but about love.

Being good parents means striving to be the best role models for our children while giving them the best guidance. If we are ready to do this, then we are ready to start a family. Love, intimacy and marriage should not be thought of as an experiment, but a noble and serious undertaking that requires commitment and wisdom.

Parents' Duties to their Children

Parents have a duty to take good care of their children, to give them love and affection and to lead them through the path of morality as set by the teachings of the Lord Buddha. In short, the duties of parents are to help their children become successful and decent human beings.

There are five primary duties that a parent must do while bringing up a child:

1. Not allowing the child to do anything evil, including the killing of people and animals, stealing, sexual misconduct, lying, speaking foul language, drinking alcohol and engaging in self-destructive behaviour.

2. Teaching the child to be established in virtue, for example, charitable giving, observing *The Five Precepts* and cultivation of the mind.

3. Ensuring that the child is properly educated.

4. Guiding the child to the right path in the careful selection of a spouse.

5. Passing on inheritances to the child.

Children's Duties to their Parents

A parent's greatest joy lies in knowing the fact that their children are grateful to them, that they follow their guidance, get a good education, are successful at work and are respected by others. Every parent wants his or her children to be good and virtuous human beings.

Children should show their gratitude to parents by living a virtuous life, showing good respect to them, speaking to them in a nice and warm fashion, and taking good care of them. Children should never hold a grudge against their parents, regardless of their shortcomings.

Parents can set a good example for their children by caring for their own ageing parents. When we take care of our parents, we should do so without expectation of anything in return. We already owe our parents a tremendous debt for giving us life in a human form, for bringing us up and for giving us an education among other things.

We should try to be self-sufficient and not count on our parents for support, even if they are wealthy. Their wealth belongs to them. They can choose to spend their money in whichever way they like. We should not regard their wealth as our own simply because we are related. We should earn a living for ourselves and create our own wealth. Any inheritances given to us by our parents should be considered as an extra gift.

If parents give their children their wealth, but the children have not built a good base of merit to sustain it, it will eventually be depleted and soon disappear no matter how much wealth is given to them. One who is void of merit is also void of wealth. This is set by *The Law of Kamma*.

Human life is made up of physical and spiritual components, such as the body and mind. Our fathers and mothers contributed the elements for our physical form, while our mind is our own. In a way, we can say that our bodies belong to our parents since they are our progenitors.

Our body is a gift from our parents and we should honour our parents by treating this 'gift' with respect and care. We should use our bodies for only worthy deeds and avoid unworthy ones. We should not allow our bodies to be contaminated by intoxicants such as alcohol, cigarettes or drugs. If we use our bodies to perform more good deeds and increase our purity, our parents will share the benefits of our good deeds too. This is another way to show our gratitude to them.

Unbreakable Bonds

The bond between a husband and wife can be broken; but the bond between parents and children is unbreakable even through death. Even if we do not know who our parents are (due to certain circumstances), we still owe them a debt of gratitude for giving us life. Some people will treat their parents to dinner probably once in a blue moon. This is not the right thing to do as expressions of love given to parents should be done frequently.

The Lord Buddha demonstrated his gratitude to his mother, Queen Sirimahamaya, after her death by ascending to see her in heaven and present to her and other angels with his *Dhamma* sermon. Upon receiving the Lord Buddha's sermon, his mother became enlightened as a *Sotapanna* (Stream-Enterer), one who has attained the first level of holiness.

While we cannot yet be like Lord Buddha, we can repay our deceased parents in other ways. We learn that the merits we accrued can be dedicated or transmitted to the deceased and improve their spiritual conditions in the after world. We need to practice a habit of dedicating merits to our deceased parents and relatives as a form of gratitude for all that they have done for us.

The loving bond we share in life, as husband and wife or as parents and children, continues even after death. If our love is deep, it should even transcend death. Some people live their lives on earth filled with mistakes and unworthy deeds. After they pass away, their bad *kamma* may cause them to end up in the unhappy realms where they endure tremendous sufferings. The good *kamma* created by the merits that we perform can act as a positive energy that can be transmitted to the deceased in order to help improve their spiritual conditions. This is a means of expressing loving kindness to the deceased.

The Heavenly Family

The family is a small but important unit in society. If each family unit is full of happiness, then the community and the nation would be stable and prosperous. It starts with the family. To achieve this stability and happiness, each family member should live a moral life – a life that is free from drugs, alcohol, gambling and adultery. If we resolve to live virtuously, even to experiment it for a period as short as one month, we will see an immediate surge in happiness within our family.

We refer to a 'heavenly family' as a '*Dhammakaya* family'. The word *Dhammakaya* means 'Body of Enlightenment', '*Dhamma* Body', 'Truth Body'. A *Dhammakaya* family does not refer only to a Buddhist family, because *Dhammakaya* exists in all human beings. It is the enlightened form, an inner refuge, which is located at the centre of the body in every person in the world. True happiness can be realised and the truth of life is understood when one attains the *Dhammakaya* within. When family members practise meditation and attain the *Dhammakaya* within, that family becomes a *Dhammakaya* family – a heavenly family.

There is an urgent need for all of us to reach the status of a *Dhammakaya* family so that our family will be full of love and happiness. We must strive to reach our inner, enlightened qualities or else our existence is not worthwhile. We may doubt whether it is possible that we may possess an enlightened form within ourselves. One way to confront this doubt is through meditation.

All serenity and peace begins at the centre of the body when the mind is still and void of all thoughts. When we can calm the mind and bring it to a completely still state, a supreme sense of happiness will spread throughout our body and radiate outward to encompass our family. If each member practises meditation daily, it is possible to achieve the 'heavenly family' state before long.

In the time of the Buddha, one example of a *Dhammakaya* family was the Anathapindika family. Everyone in Anathapindika's household – from his wife, children and servants – all attended the temple, listened to the *Dhamma*, and lived a life of purity. On Buddhist Holy Days, everyone observed *The Eight Precepts*, even the youngest children. They all reached their *Dhammakaya* within. This is an example of a heavenly family.

Any family that has alcohol, cigarettes and other unwholesome items within the house will find it difficult to become a heavenly family. The atmosphere of the house will be saturated with the offensive smell of tobacco smoke and alcohol, together with the noise from all the yelling and the fighting going on in the house.

Human beings must live in a wholesome environment in order to prosper. A good person cannot get out of the house to perform good deeds if his safety is threatened by gang members or drunkards. It is important that we cultivate our minds, practise good deeds and work together to become moral people.

A mind that is cultivated and purified is a superior mind. A superior mind makes good decisions. When our minds are at peace, we are at peace. Our families and our surroundings will be peaceful too. Meditation is indeed a very important part of a person's life and should be practised by everyone in the family. Love, understanding and cooperation will arise at home and will spread to the community and the nation. World peace starts with inner peace. A heavenly family will grow into a heavenly country and as more and more people learn to meditate, a heavenly world will not be beyond reach.

Chapter 5
The Ultimate Love

Accepting Change

Many people realise that once they are married, marriage is not what they have imagined it to be. Their expectations may have been influenced by idealistic love stories from movies and television, where lovers are handsome, beautiful and loving. But in reality, good things do not last forever. Our lovers, who once used to be handsome and beautiful, now become old and are no longer good-looking. The face and the body that you once admired have become wrinkled, obese or bald. This is the nature of the physical world where nothing is permanent and everything is subjected to change.

Unrealistic expectations are reasons why human beings fall in and out of love so quickly. In the face of such transient and unreliable emotions, it is necessary for us to search for a pure and lasting kind of love.

Where there is love, there is suffering. Suffering is caused by attachment and desire. The more love and yearning we have, the more suffering we face because we will share the concerns, worries and pains of the people we love. If our loved ones become sick, we also feel their pain. If we are separated from our loved ones, we feel the pain from missing and worrying about each other.

Marriage may fulfil the need for companionship, but it cannot fulfil our need for perfect happiness. Perfect happiness does not come from outside sources. Even if someone gives us money, a luxury car, a nice house and all that we desire, we will still be unable to feel complete happiness. The true

state of happiness cannot be given to us by others. It has to be earned by the individual who wishes to obtain it. Believe it or not, this perfect state of happiness lies within our inner selves.

All human beings are born into this world as individuals before coming together to form a family. When we depart from this world, we will leave individually as well. Our children do not truly belong to us because we do not own their minds. We can raise them but we cannot control how and what they think and do.

A pregnant woman can support the life of her unborn child until the child enters the world. Although she may feed, raise, teach and do everything for the child, she cannot expect him or her to be everything she wants him or her to be. Sometimes the child would obey her but other times he or she would not. As the child grows older, he or she might even become completely opposite of what the mother wants him or her to be.

Each person has his own thoughts, speech and actions that no other person can control. For this reason, our child is never truly 'ours'. No one in the world, be it husband, wife or child belongs fully to another person. The only person we own is ourselves. Therefore, we should treat ourselves well with good discipline and moral values.

Life Has Its Limitations

A married life has its limitations. Compare a fish that lives in a bowl to a fish

that lives in the ocean or compare a caged bird to a bird that can fly freely in the sky. While each lifestyle has its benefits and disadvantages, it cannot be denied that having a family does confine our life and limit our freedom. We will not always have time to pursue meditation, do the things we enjoy or pursue our hobbies when our spouse and children demand our time and attention.

Living a layman's life makes it difficult to practise all the virtues that are required if one wishes to become an *Arahant* (an enlightened being who is free from defilements and no longer subjected to rebirths or reach *Nibbana*). A layman can attain a certain level of spiritual achievement, but those who wish to reach enlightenment need to be ordained as a monk, nun, or practice a life of complete purity.

Many couples get married because they feel the mutual desire to start a family. However, as we have come to realise, life partners do not share only one goal but many. Some have made pursuing *Perfections* and keeping *The Precepts* as their primary life goal. Therefore, as life partners who are in pursuit of *Perfections* together, they should thoroughly consider how they will live their lives if one of them decides to live a life of chastity.

In Buddhist history, there are many examples of different couples and how each pursued *Perfections*. Visakha is one example. In her pursuit of *Perfections*, she was at the level of a *Sotapanna* (Stream-Enterer), one who attained the first stage of holiness. As a married woman, she performed the duties of a good wife and had 20 children (10 sons and 10 daughters). She understood the roles of a husband and a wife according to *The Precepts*, virtues and the law that valued monogamy. She accepted that as a human being and a wife, she had to live with certain responsibilities and limitations, even though she was a *Sotapanna* (Stream-Enterer). Although she wanted to live a celibate life, she ultimately could not do so in that lifetime.

Another example is Pipphali and Bhaddakapilani, who were husband and wife for a period of over 100,000 consecutive lives. In one lifetime, they were born to parents who wished for the two to be married. Although they both preferred to live chaste lives, they agreed to the marriage in order to appease their parents but lived together for many years as if they were siblings. When their parents passed away, they both ordained to be a monk and nun. Each gave the other blessings as they departed to pursue *Nibbana*.

There is also the story of Lady Uttra, who was married and also wished to perform merits. She asked her husband for permission to perform merits for seven days, but he told her that he would be lonely without her. Lady Uttra then arranged for Lady Sirima, a beautiful prostitute to temporarily take care of her husband, during which time Lady Uttra was able to perform merits and live a holy life.

While Lady Uttra's example is an extreme case, we and our partner must consider which lifestyle is appropriate for us both without causing bitterness and resentment and the sin of adultery. This is very difficult for some couples, but more feasible for others.

If we wish to live a life of chastity, the best and easiest path would be to make that

important decision before getting married. However, if we are already married, we need to realise we have already promised to take on a role and that if we choose to live chastely later on, the decision must involve our partner in order to preserve the marriage.

This issue is a major one and it can cause many intense conflicts between couples if both do not choose to live celibate lives. One solution is to select specific dates to observe *The Eight Precepts*, such as on Buddhist Holy days or on birthdays. This compromise allows both parties to meet obligations as well as observe *The Precepts*.

When the Lord Buddha was still Prince Siddhattha, he had everything – a beautiful wife, a son, wealth, servants, power and prestige. However, these things never led him to the highest happiness. He walked away from his family and all material comforts to assume the life of an ascetic. In the end, he reached enlightenment and entered into *Nibbana*, free from all cares and defilements.

A married life can offer many comforts such as companionship and children, but in the end it distracts one from the ultimate goal of attaining *Nibbana*. Many people mistakenly think that being unmarried means insecurity or loneliness, but in actuality, an unmarried person lives a life with the freedom and opportunity to pursue *Nibbana* wholeheartedly.

Loving Oneself

Before we can love anyone, we need to love ourselves first. Loving oneself and being

selfish are two separate and distinct things. Selfishness means contaminating oneself with unwholesome and deluded thoughts, speech and actions, because one is only thinking of oneself. It shows we have no love for other people. In contrast, if we love ourselves, we would wish only goodness and happiness for ourselves.

In order to achieve this, we have to create an environment of happiness by purifying our thoughts, speech and actions. We should perform good deeds with our bodies, minds and speech. Everything that passes through our senses can be both good and bad; therefore, we must be selective and decide what we choose to pass through our bodies and minds. The decision is entirely up to us.

Meditation is the only means that can lead one to the attainment of inner refuge, a refuge that one can turn to during harsh times, and also in the final moments of his or her lives. Even after death, we can still rely on it. It is our constant refuge until we reach the ultimate goal. The person who loves himself must take care of himself. It is impossible for others to be responsible for us.

When we suffer, we experience the pain ourselves – it cannot be transferred to others. Each time we are sick, the illness is within ourselves – other people can only console us. If we overcome that illness, we can appreciate the fact that we did so with our own effort.

Although each and every one of us has a family and forms a part of society, we must realise that ultimately we create joy or sadness through our own actions. If we love ourselves, then we should make the effort to increase the pureness within us.

Let go of our worries. Ignore the things that bother us or make us unhappy. Purify our minds through regular practice of meditation. Keep a happy and upbeat attitude. Along with the capacity that we have in us to love our husband, wife, children and friends, more deeply, we will gain happiness in ourselves, like a sun that shines with its own radiance.

Universal Love

As the sky withdraws its rain, the colourful rainbows appear to bridge heaven and earth. Rich in a variety of colours, the world is beautified with this natural ornamentation.

Likewise, the differences of mankind are of one nature. However, if we practise meditation consistently until we achieve the holistic meditation experience and look through the bright light that emerges from our mental vision, we will see the hidden inner similarity otherwise known as *Dhammakaya*.

Upon this meditative discovery beyond the external existence, we will be able to see and understand life clearly. Then, our hearts will brim with only pure love and happiness. We will no longer crave for love from others, but become the source of powerful unconditional love which is complete in itself. This is 'universal love' that can be extended to all others. It is a positive energy in our minds that cherishes loving kindness, compassion and goodwill, without the contamination of lust and defilement.

Universal love is so powerful that it goes beyond personal interest. It is the kind of love that the Lord Buddha had after his enlightenment. Although he had accompanied Princess Bimba for many lifetimes to pursue *Perfections*, he could finally make a decision to let go of his personal affection and enter a state of ordination. He persevered in meditation practice until he managed to attain enlightenment which symbolises the extinction of all sufferings. Subsequently, he had great compassion in teaching as well as training both human and deities in the attainment of enlightenment, so that they can liberate themselves just like he did.

Even for Princess Bimba, his former wife, and Prince Rahula, his son, who had spent many lifetimes with the *Bodhisatta* as a virtuous family, the Lord Buddha returned and brought them the precious teaching of *Dhamma* with his universal love. Princess Bimba and Prince Rahula also decided to ordain and practised the *Dhamma* until they became *Arahants*, marking the very end of their long journey in *samsara*, the cycle of existence.

Thus, the Lord Buddha is the true role model for universal love that we should take into account and follow accordingly. His story denotes that universal love is the final form of love that everyone can achieve. It is the kind of love that we should also seek for in our lives in order to receive true happiness in return.

What is Life?

What is life?
A fantasy lived half asleep
Which disappears at dawn,
Or time we borrow but cannot keep
Soon to be repaid with interest?
Life so far has been merely a reflection upon water
Dissolving into fragments and then nothingness.
Why bind ourselves
To that which we cannot alter?
The only rock amongst the confusion
Is created by a mind infused with purity
Whose eye sees with clarity
Whose perception reaches to the centre
Where only joy and peacefulness may enter.
Then life is Finally lived as it should be,
Filled with light until infinity.

Luang Phaw Dhammajayo

A Fair Way to Love

As you now grasp the concept of preserving love and uplifting the high-spirited love to the elevated level of inner love, called lovely love, I shall introduce you to some real-life examples, kindly contributed by our fellow friends who had struggled with delusive perceptions of love. By fine-tuning their concept of love to the one in line with the natural truth – the *Dhamma* – and importing the knowledge into everyday practice, these individuals have come to attain 'the fair way to love'.

The following pages contain a series of accounts of individuals who are on their marvellous journeys of attaining lovely love: married couples whose towering walls of cultural and religious differences melted away upon the warmth of the *Dhamma* applied at home; an expatriate housewife whose ecstatic enlightenment on inner love by the power of deep meditative tranquillity rooted out her agony of possessive affection and sowed the seed of a life-long relationship; a self-indulgent wife who woke up to realise the meaning of her life through a cognitive meditation voyage which catalysed a makeover for her marriage for a harmonious family; and a disappointed love-seeker whose spiritual rebirth into the life in the realm of truth, completed her quest with lasting delight from the acquired wisdom of inner love. Hopefully, these inspirational real-life accounts will become an example to others in their pursuit for endless love in their lives.

Testimony 1

Mrs Anchalee Nathanson, USA

"His teachings, above all, instill in us the intellect to cultivate inner, rather than extrinsic, love. The fully-fledged inner love shall safeguard the spiritual perfection of one's soul, with no vain struggle for extrinsic addition. With the revelation of life's truth, blissful life is attainable even by one single soul because true happiness can only shine from within."

My name is Anchalee Nathanson and I am married to a Jewish American whose name is Michael Nathanson. We have two adorable sons – Ilan and Joshua. Our family lives in New

Jersey, USA. Surprisingly indeed, the proven happy marriage formula I am sharing with you was kindly shared by our beloved Luang Phaw Dhammajayo.

Here is my story – a story of two lovebirds that voyaged on an overseas quest for love and sealed the beautiful bond with a marriage union. Sadly, our hearts were divided by the coastline because of emerging differences and our love eventually faded into the background.

Both my husband and I have the type of character that firmly upholds self-justice. Unlike my husband, I came across an opportune chance to learn about, contemplate and apprehend Luang Phaw's saying that 'marriage' is indeed a join-up to create greater family joy together. In achieving so, couples should continue to say sweet and loving words to each other continually everyday even after the honeymoon stage is over, despite a deepening familiarity that one has towards the other over time.

Years ago, when we were newly-weds, my husband would return from work every Friday with a bouquet of beautiful roses in his hand for me. As time flew by, the bouquet size got smaller until there was only a single rose. I passed a sarcastic remark one day by saying: "Honey, I noticed that I get fewer and fewer roses these days – till there's only one left for me today. Well, next time I might get only the stamp" To my words, he replied with a shy smile. Surprisingly, I received a big gorgeous rose bouquet the following Friday, which I feel symbolizes apologies and reconciliation after a decade of marriage life. A rose bouquet with his same old shy smile ends every argument that happened between us on the previous night.

Luang Phaw Dhammajayo shared his words of wisdom on a couple's life, which was to: "Smile always, stay serene and be subtle-minded and then his heart will surrender". These words inculcated strength into my inner spirit and helps me remove my temper, leaving me a calmer person who always beams with delight each time I receive his vibrant roses.

In the past, I was accustomed to letting the bitterness and hatred run deep for days and even came up with clever ways to retaliate. Such resentful preoccupation turned me into nothing but an emotional freak with a perpetually frowning face.

My incorporation of the happy marriage formula – 'Smile, be serene and be subtle-minded' – into everyday practice brought about a major change, which my husband in particular noticed and felt. He appreciated the effort that I was putting in towards making our marriage work and eventually one day, he 'surrendered' his heart. My husband approached me with a request for me to pledge a life-long commitment: "You have to grow old with me", he said. The request indeed was testimony to his unquestionable love and deep longing for me.

Michael was a man of high stature – he was well-groomed, smart and successful, career wise and financial wise – and he is hence popular with the opposite sex. I am just an ordinary woman, who has had my personality carved to near perfection by Luang Phaw's words.

"Do things in the right place at the right time. Just like a house that comprises several rooms for different purposes, a complete family life is made up of several respective roles that need to be fulfilled. To be an ideal wife, you simply have to be accomplished and competent in all the roles required of you. For instance, let your family be served with the best meal at the dinner table; let your husband be relaxed while he is in the living room and engage in a light-hearted conversation with him to ease his soul." Upon hearing this advice, I smiled with relief at myself for discovering the sought-after solution to my marital problem.

Having a string of responsibilities such as juggling time between raising two kids and arranging new home purchases on top of adjusting to a lifestyle in an unfamiliar social environment, I was busy almost everyday and the heightened stress loosened my grip on emotional expressions. Unfortunately, my firstborn, Ilan, the focal destination of all affections, had to suffer and was most adversely affected by my mood swings.

I remember crying my eyes out beholding his soft skin covered with weals following the blows that were of my doings. The abject pang of guilt in my heart, together with the overwhelming self-doubt I had towards my parenting abilities, woke me up to tackle these angry hands of mine. The idea of practicing meditation as a soul-pacifier crossed and afterwards stayed on my mind. Besides just meditating, I embarked on the habit of donating as well as observing Buddhist precepts.

The religious differences, of both my husband and I, triggered frequent arguments. He expressed his disappointment by saying: "You betrayed me" or "You are not my sole mate anymore". These cut me through, but my conscience nevertheless objected to subserviently relinquishing my pursuance of the *Dhamma*, the ultimate purpose in a human's life. In an attempt to ease the situation, I adopted Luang Phaw's approach to domestic harmony which was to 'identify the mutual interest whilst bridging the gap of difference to alleviate the conflict'.

Both my husband and I had the common interest of concentrating on our kids as well as on our own reciprocal affection. The gap between us lies in our religious differences and I anticipated that my endeavor to meditate could be the key bridge to bring us closer together. One day eventually, my perseverance was repaid when my husband approached me for an instruction in meditation.

Even more conducive to the success of my ongoing effort to bridge the gap was Luang Phaw's initiative of the Inner Dreams Kindergarten, the satellite broadcasting program whereby the Buddha's teachings on the cycle of Karma – the underlying mechanism for the material consequences of virtuous and vicious deeds – reached audiences around the globe. I myself too came to a genuine understanding of how things that went around manage to come around through this very channel. Not only has Luang Phaw's crystal clear elaboration simplified the sophisticated knowledge, his preaching surrounding the concept of unconditional, boundless and inclusive love was also paramount.

Luang Phaw's benign compassion to people, reflected in his pioneering deployment of several intuitive techniques in *Dhamma* education on the satellite program, permeates into hearts all over the world – including my two sons. Both Ilan and Joshua feel closely connected to Luang Phaw despite the geographical space that exists between them. His teachings, above all, instill in us the intellect to cultivate inner, rather than extrinsic, love. The fully-fledged inner love shall safeguard the spiritual perfection of one's soul, with no vain struggle for extrinsic addition. With the revelation of life's truth, blissful life is attainable even by one single soul because true happiness can only shine from within.

Testimony 2

Mrs Phady Chanthabouasy, USA

"Whenever I start to get irritated, my husband would say: "My dear, we should not let our temper get to us. Let's smile just like how Luang Phaw teaches us to." We still implement Luang Phaw's teachings, which is to love simultaneously and be angry at different times."

My name is Phady Chanthabouasy. I am a 54-year-old Laotian-American living in Oregon, USA. I have been living in the US for more than 30 years and my husband is also a Laotian-American. He works as a helicopter pilot in the army. I first installed a DMC satellite dish in 2003 with the recommendation from a member of the Seattle Meditation Center. At the beginning, I was disinterested and replied that I had no money. The person assured me that I could borrow the system for three months without any charge, and I could return it if I did not like it.

The very first time I turned on the DMC program, I heard Luang Phaw Dhammajayo saying: "My dear, you must endure in the meditation practice because we haven't seen each other for so many lifetimes already." After I heard these words, I cried suddenly. Ever since then, I have been watching the DMC program consistently. If I miss the program for a single day, I would feel uncomfortable.

After three months, I decided not to return the satellite dish system. In addition, I also helped to convince the others to get their own systems. Previously, I always got upset and had quarrels with my husband. We could not converse smoothly, although we speak the same language.

My husband loved to consume liquor. He did not go to the temple, no matter which one. To make it worse, he even questioned me each time I go to the temple to make merits. He would ask: "What are making merits like?" Listening to his question, I was angered and responded immediately that I disliked his question.

Although we are a couple, our paths are torn apart. This spurred me on to make a resolution for myself to make my husband accompany me to make merits at the temple. Each time, I chanted: "With the power of merit

I had made for 30 years, may my husband, Somsy, go to make merit with me at the temple." Until I viewed the DMC program and had a chance to join the first lady-meditation-retreat program in Azusa, California, I have practiced meditation consistently. I started by inviting the Great Master to enshrine in my abdomen and recite the mantra '*Samma Arahang*' repeatedly. I think of nothing else and keep my mind still with the image of the Great Master. Soon, I would see his face similar to the picture that I received from the temple. Then, I continued to recite the mantra.

Later on, I saw the golden image of the Great Master arising within my body. As I looked through the middle of this image, I saw a white and soft light glowing. It was hard to describe in words, but the light did not irritate my eyes. I felt happy and did not want to leave my meditation session. I enjoyed it so much that I continued to practice regularly.

Whenever my husband saw me practicing meditation, he would tease me "Why do you have to meditate? Isn't it better if you have a nap?" When I was to go to the temple, he teased "Why do you have to go to the temple, better stay at home," and "What is merit? How does it look like?" But, at that time, I had the answers, so I replied calmly and said: "My dear, merit is the brightness that emanates from within. If you don't believe me, you can try meditation for yourself." Then, I called the teaching monk who taught me at the temple, telling him that I would not attend the ceremony because I had introduced meditation to my husband.

That day, I spoke to my husband politely, using all the flowery language, in order to convince him to meditate. I told him, "My dear, let's practice meditation. Just five or ten minutes. If you love me, please, just spare me ten minutes." So, my husband agreed.

I coached my husband gradually. I told him to close his eyes, relax and focus his mind within his abdomen. Then, I turned the meditation instruction tape of Luang Phaw for him. During meditation, I opened my eyes to see how he was doing. I was surprised that he could sit still for more than five or ten minutes and that he could meditate for a long time even though he never practiced it before. Ironically, I was the one who introduced meditation to him, but I opened my eyes first!

Even after an hour has passed, my husband still sat still in meditation, and after two hours of silence, he opened his eyes and told me: "I just relaxed myself and listened to Luang Phaw's guidance, I recited '*Samma Arahang*' in my mind, and soon, I saw brightness within my abdomen. It did not irritate my eyes, and I was very happy. I did not want to leave my seat." Since then, my husband has been practicing meditation, and he could see a very clear crystal ball, like a shampoo bubble that is bright and rounded. After looking through the middle of the crystal ball, the crystal ball kept expanding and this made him truly happy.

Now, my husband believes that merit really does exist. He also confirmed that whatever Luang Phaw Dhammajayo said was true. He is now my coach because I see only brightness. My husband already saw the source of brightness which was the crystal sphere. He told me: "My dear, listen to me, take it easy and relax. Don't think of anything. Not the past. Not the future. The future hasn't arrived yet. Just keep your mind still at the present, and you will be able to see a clear and bright crystal sphere. As you keep observing, it would expand. Simply relax, and you will see it by yourself."

Nowadays, we live in harmony and we have a good understanding of one another. We are two individuals on the same journey leading to heaven on earth and the afterlife. People are amazed that we no longer quarrel. We do not fight anymore, and my husband has quit smoking and drinking. We converse with much more understanding now.

Whenever I start to get irritated, my husband would say: "My dear, we should not let our temper get to us. Let's smile just like how Luang Phaw teaches us to." We still implement

Luang Phaw's teachings to 'love simultaneously and be angry at different times.'

These days, my husband and I always perform chanting and practice meditation together regularly. The best part is that he no longer wants to go out roaming, but would rather stay home to watch the DMC program with me.

Testimony 3

Mrs Sawangjit Jacschke, Germany

❝I have loved myself even more after all that had happened and discovered an important lesson from my experience, which is to love myself before others!❞

My name is Sawangjit Jacschke and I am 36 years old. My husband's name is Hanswerner Jacschke and he is living in Peine, Germany. I discovered Wat Phra Dhammakaya in December 2005 when a fellow invited me to practise meditation at the meditation centre in Germany. Following that, I decided to install the DMC satellite dish in my home.

Prior to this, I was constantly moody and easily agitated. This was attributed to my health conditions. I had my uterus removed due to tumour growth when I was 16 years old. It has also caused me to experience emotional fluctuation, dizziness, fainting and have a bad temperament.

My husband understood my character very well. Whenever he did something that irritated me, I would complain and grumble non-stop, irrespective of any good reasons. My rules were simple, they were: (1) I was always right, and (2) If you didn't understand, check out rule number one.

Sometimes, I become mad and throw things around but my husband never took it seriously because he knew that he would not end up getting hurt. He would shake his head and say: "Huh! Why are you so cruel? Women are all the same." After that, he would turn to me and ask: "Do you feel better now? Can you stop being so crazy?"

Another problem that I faced was jealousy. I was a very jealous and possessive person by nature. I was suspicious of my husband's whereabouts, even though I know that he would leave the house for work from seven in the morning and return at about ten at night everyday. If he returned home later than ten at night, I would interrogate him immediately. This became our marital problem as he always claimed that he was not involved in anything other than his work.

Ever since we were married, I had been suspicious of my husband's actions every single day. Whenever I complained at night, he would already have fallen asleep. In the end, I had to stay awake alone in bed and wait for him to wake up the next morning in order to express how I really feel. But in the end, he will usually have a good sleep while I was the only one who was all stressed up.

One day, I decided to find a way to spy on him and find out why he kept returning home so late. I laid out many plans so that I can discover the truth. One fine morning, I told him that I would like to work at his company. Indeed, I had a hidden agenda that he was not aware of. His company was recruiting new employees then and I took the opportunity to apply for a position there.

In the beginning, my husband did not want me to go because he knew my character very well. At work, I followed him closely and my jealousy grew. I caused trouble and suffered as a result. Interestingly, my husband was never affected. He laughed and felt proud that I got jealous because it meant that I loved him a lot. Despite my husband telling me repeatedly to let go of those ill thoughts, I grew anxious and eventually suffered from insomnia.

I couldn't help thinking a lot; sometimes I kept thinking until midnight. One sleepless night, I decided to try meditating. I just sat and let time go by, waiting for myself to feel sleepy. I did not expect anything and my husband was already asleep. Soon, I grew sleepy but I could faintly recognise a crystal sphere arising in my abdomen. The soft sphere was glowing and its size was similar to that of a yellow full moon. I felt so blissful as I have never experienced this before. I continued to meditate and smiled peacefully alone on the bed. During my work each day, I would make it a point to go for a short break to close my eyes in order to see the crystal sphere in my body. It is so amazing that sometimes, I feel like I am radiating a glow myself. Whenever I experience this, I can feel my mind getting clearer and I would feel extremely happy.

Ever since I tried meditating, I have never skipped meditation for a single day. Presently, I could see the *Dhammakaya* within the crystal sphere. The colour is a light sky blue. In the beginning, the *Dhammakaya* is tiny. It would expand within me and extend beyond as I meditate. Now, whenever I have problems, I would close my eyes, still my mind and think of the *Dhammakaya*.

Now, I am no longer suspicious of my husband. He is surprised at the change in my behaviour. He is now afraid that I would leave him alone because I spend more time practising meditation. With meditation, I do not get jealous anymore. If I did not meditate, I would have gone crazy and buckled under all the stress that I was facing.

Once, I told my husband that I could live alone. I told him that I do not depend on him to live my life. Instead, my life is within me at the centre of my body. My husband asked if I really meant it and laughed cheerfully. I have loved myself even more after all that had happened and discovered an important lesson from my experience, which is to love myself before others!

Testimony 4

**Mrs Taweeporn Tansanguan,
Thailand**

"Presently, our married life is like that of angels, which differs greatly from the past. In the past, people say we are like a couple that comprises an angel and an ogress. I have learnt a valuable lesson and have become aware that meditation can create such great happiness. It has the power to change the person's life for good to an extent that they would have never expected before."

My name is Taweeporn Tansanguan. I am a housewife living in Chachoengsao province. I first visited Wat Phra Dhammakaya in 2003 with a good friend (*kalayanamitta*) who invited me to join the meditation retreat at Panawat Meditation Park. This incident has poured light into my life and has led me to the right path.

My husband is a foreman in a private company. He is so well-paid that I do not have to work. He gives me 300,000 baht every month without asking me how I spend the money.

Once, my relative sold his pub to me and I ran the business myself. Every day, during opening hours, I drank with customers, and even after the shop was closed, I still continued drinking with my neighbours. My business eventually failed because I always gave the customers free drinks after they bought their first drink.

When I was drunk, I did not know what I was doing. Once, I lost my senses and promised to give a woman my room in a condominium. The next day, when I regained my conscience, I had to transfer the ownership of my condominium to her reluctantly and paid for the fee myself because she could not afford it. My husband never blamed me for doing this. He told me to do as I wished. After I finished the transferring process, I came back and drank in the evening as usual. My husband teased me by saying: "What next will you give your friend today?"

Later on, my friend persuaded me to invest in a karaoke business. I spent millions of baht on this project. Again, the business did not succeed because I treated my customers instead of selling the service to them. Each night when I got drunk, I would roam around the same night until morning. I was nicknamed a 'ghost' because I rested during the daytime and woke up at night to drink. I spent more than a thousand baht a day leading this kind of life. My new business lasted only two months before I had to sell it cheaply and lost a large sum of money. My husband advised me not to invest in any business because it would be better to save money by staying at home.

I believed him and stayed at home making my own alcoholic drinks. I brewed two big jars of alcohol. One jar was readily available for me to drink when the other ran out. I drank everyday, each time a mugful. Alcohol seemed like a normal and common drink to me. I also bottled it and gave it to merchants in the nearby market. When the merchants got drunk, I invited them to the karaoke party in my house.

My husband did not discourage me. Sometimes, he also joined our parties and sang with me, but he never drank alcohol. When I got drunk, he washed, powdered and perfumed me before taking me to sleep in our air-conditioned bedroom. He was always kind to me but I just took him for granted. I treated him badly, gave him orders and played tricks on him.

Once, a drunk friend of mine followed me home and told my husband that he wanted me. Crying, my husband replied that he would never let me go and affirmed that I was his love. However, if I wanted to go myself, he would not stop me. It was up to me to make my own decision. Upon hearing this, I decided to chase the drunkard out of my house. I realised then that no matter how much I had let him down, he was never mad at me. He said to my mother and my son that he did not cry at his father's death but he cried because of my bad behaviour.

When I was out in the car with him, he would play the song 'Someday you will know what it feels like without me.' Behind his spectacles, I saw tears trickling down his cheeks. This sight is one that still remains fresh in my memory.

My husband often makes merit and always offers food to monks. But for me, it is different. Every year on Buddhist Lent Day, I take my friends to a temple to pray and observe the precepts. In the morning, I requested for precepts but when it reached noon, I went home and continued to drink alcohol. I knew it was not right, but I did not know why it was wrong. Sometimes, after offering food to monks, I did not pour ceremonial water immediately but had some drinks first.

Apart from being an alcoholic, I was also a lottery addict. Every fortnight, I bought lottery that cost about seven to ten thousand baht, but I never won any prize. My husband told me to save this amount of money in a bank. He said that it would be like I won the lottery prize when the results were drawn because all the money that I have saved all this while will still be with me.

Back then, I was a ferocious and ill-tempered person. Everybody was afraid of me, including my mother and my husband. Once, I struck my sister's head with a chopping knife. Her fillet was broken, and her head was covered with blood. I persisted and continued hitting her again with a bottle of soft drink. Her head was terribly injured and bled profusely the second time. My sister-in-law was also hit by a pair of hot tongs that burned and peeled off her skin. I also hit my brother and kicked him at his chin as he bowed before me asking me to have pity on him. He bled as a result of my kicks. No one could stop my anger. When I got angry, everybody had to listen to me. They could not argue or walk away. My husband was so afraid that I saw him shaking in fear each time I lost my temper. I asked him why he was so afraid of me. He said that when I got mad, it seemed like I was possessed by a ghost.

I lived my life this way until I went to the Panawat Meditation Park in 2003. I took my mother along with me as she was also an alcoholic. When we both listened to the sermon of Luang Phaw Dhammajayo from

DMC channel at Panawat, we then recognised the truth of life.

Meditation had the power to calm me down. When I first practised meditation, my legs ached but the pain went away as I prayed to the Great Master. My mind kept focusing on the centre of my body and I could see the light inside my stomach. I felt happy and free like I was in a vast and fresh open field. I felt like my body was covered with crystals and my stomach expanded and the light shining within me got brighter. I was filled with joy. Several hours of meditation seemed like a short time for me. I continued meditating until someone called out to me to have a meal. During meditation, I realised that there is no other happiness greater than the inner happiness which is derived from meditation. It is a really blissful moment.

Since then, my life has changed dramatically. I do not act violently nor break *The Precepts* anymore. Now, I spend time with books and meditation. Every morning and evening, I greet other people politely and pay respects to my husband every night before we go to bed. I also pay respects to my mother as often as possible and ask for her forgiveness for my past mistakes. This made my mother cry with joy. Actually, it is hard for me to greet other people first because I was never a modest person before, but after my *Dhamma* practice, I started to greet everyone including my maids. Furthermore, I share merit with my relatives and acquaintances who never saw me act kindly like this before. This surprises them a lot because they are used to seeing me furious, violent and vengeful. But now, I have changed. I have become calmer. When I get angry, I do not go on a rampage any longer.

Instead, I learn to forgive and forget. When I have conflicts with my husband, I keep quiet instead of bursting out. I will be the one who will ask for reconciliation first. In the past, the situation was very different. Whether I was right or wrong, my husband was the one who had to make peace first.

I reflected on things that happened in the past and realised that I was wrong. I used to neglect other people's opinions and feelings and even scolded and hurt them. After practising the *Dhamma*, I felt that I wanted only to do good things and say good words. These actions were done without effort. It was a 99.99 percent change. All of these are the result of meditation.

My husband asked me what happened to me during my meditation course. He said if he knew I could change to become this good, he had wished that my friend would have taken me there a long time ago. I am a lucky woman because my husband is a good man. He always forgives me no matter what happens. Our lives are much happier now.

Presently, our married life is like that of angels, which differs greatly from the past. In the past, people say we are like a couple that is comprised of an angel and an ogress. I have learnt a valuable lesson and have become aware that meditation can create such great happiness. It has the power to change the person's life for good to an extent that they would have never expected before.

Testimony 5

Ms Pornprachern Boonsungnern, USA

"When I love others, I give that person 100 percent but in turn, the hurt I get is equivalent to what I give. If I love myself, I give to myself 100 percent. In return, I receive abundant and overflowing happiness every single day and night in my life. I hope to expand and share this wondrous joy with people from all over the world."

My name is Pornprachern Boonsungnern, 49 years old and living in Nevada, USA. Both my Thai friends and foreign fellows know me for my songs 'I am another woman', 'I am Thai' and 'Must fight to win'. Although most of them praise me for my sweet voice, in reality my life is full of bitterness and sufferings.

I was born in Korat (Nakornratchasima province). I lost my mother since I was young and my father is paralyzed. I have many siblings in my family and we have to take care of one another and share the love and warmth together. Our family was very poor; once, we had to scour the garbage pile for food and we had to walk to school barefooted because we could not afford shoes.

My life got better when I attended a singing contest in 1985 and clinched the top singing award at Siam Konlakarn. Other singers such as Berd (Thongchai McIntai) also attended the contest that year. After my win, I successfully released my own album. Although I was secure about myself physically, I could not find any solution to solve the problems that resided in my heart. The problem that I faced was my continued failure in love. I never got along with my boyfriend. I wished to have endless love but it was always shortlived and this eventually depleted me of energy. I often asked myself why I have to go through all this pain and why no one truly loved me although I had given them my love and took care of them wholeheartedly. At the end of the day, I was always the one who ended up in heartbreak.

Fortunately, I did not let myself down for too long. I restrained myself and gathered my strength to persevere. When I felt really sad, I would tell myself each time to continue fighting and win. To solve the problems, I would go to Buddhist temples and make merits.

If I had huge problems, I would make huge merits. This was how I knew about Wat Phra Dhammakaya in 2001, under the guidance of a good fellow (*kalyanamitta*) from Korat who suggested that I contribute for the casting of an individual Buddha Image.

In 2002, I moved to the US. I wanted to do merit, so I did it at the temple near my house until I came across one of the many branches of Wat Phra Dhammakaya temple that was situated in Virginia. I met a teacher-monk and I conversed with him joyously. One year later, I went to the Seattle Meditation Center to offer sustenance. There, I met the same monk who had previously taught me in Virginia. He told me about the DMC Program via the satellite system and showed me the program. In the program, I saw two adorable girls, Naomi and Pang, reciting the Pali language. I was very much impressed and told myself: "These little kids can speak the Pali Language. Why can't I? I have to learn it and upgrade myself".

Since that day, I decided to make a change for myself by installing the DMC Satellite dish. I studied the *Dhamma* from DMC everyday. Each time I watched Luang Phaw, I became more impressed by his great teachings about the *Dhamma*. In the past, I did not like to listen to the *Dhamma* at all. Normally, I would just go back home after I have made donations, but now I really look forward to listen to the *Dhamma*. I do not feel bored at all because I am very happy and love to hear about the *Dhamma*.

After that, I listened to Luang Phaw's voice each time I meditate. If I have enough time, I will meditate twice a day. When I drive, I sing the praising song and chant the morning verses until my car reaches my work place. Then, I make a wish to Luang Pu Wat Pak Nam's (Phramongkolthepmuni's) picture. In the evening, after I get home from work, I meditate before I go to bed.

For the first time, I sat down and visualized a crystal ball according to Luang Phaw's teachings. I did not see anything but darkness inside. Later, I just closed my eyes and did nothing at all till I felt my body disappear and my mind coming to a standstill. It felt as though I was in an open space. I felt free, happy and comfortable as if nobody was around. Following that, each time I meditated, I discovered that I obtained the feeling of immense happiness that was impossible to describe in words. Through meditation, I fell deeper in love with myself and I can safely say that this love felt like the truest love of my life. When I love others, I give that person 100 percent but in turn, the hurt I get is equivalent to what I give. If I love myself, I give to myself 100 percent. In return, I receive abundant and overflowing happiness every single day and night in my life and I hope to expand and share this wondrous joy with people from all over the world.

When I feel peaceful, everything feels great and every problem can be solved, even the serious ones. I am very proud to discover Wat Phra Dhammakaya, Luang Phaw Dhammajayo and every meditator that I know of. I have become a better person from the way I look at things now, rather than in the past. I tell myself that whatever happens, it is always for the good of everyone. At least, I can tell myself to 'take it easy and not cry'.

Now, I always tell myself that in order to be a good Buddhist, I need to have a firm heart. Even during my show, the audience always offer drinks to me. I respond to them by saying: "I am sorry but I do not drink." Many times they have urged me by asking me to drink to their honor. If I refuse, they will say: "So, does it mean that you do not honor me?" I answered proudly, "I give you an honor by sitting with you, but I do not drink because I hold *The Precepts* and I am a real Buddhist who does not drink and smoke. If you would like to talk to me, please do not urge me to drink anymore." I think that real Buddhists have to stand up to do the right things and follow morality strictly.

Every time, before my stage show, I pray to praise Phramongkolthepmuni to recall him and Master Nun Chand. My highest achievement was when I had the chance to sing a beautiful song entitled 'What is Life?' written by Luang Phaw Dhammajayo. It is a really beautiful song, and it helps me let go of the troubles that I am facing. I am not concerned about loving others anymore, but concerned to love myself even more.

Glossary

1. **Arahant**

   An enlightened being who is free from defilements and no longer subjected to rebirths or attained *Nibbana*.

2. **Bodhisatta**

   One who determines to be a Buddha in the future.

3. **Dhamma**

   A phenomenon when seen as an aspect of the universe, rather than identified with as personal. When capitalised, it refers to the teaching of the Buddha as contained in the scriptures or the Ultimate Truth towards which the teaching points. (In Sanskrit, it is known as '*dharma*')

4. Kalayanamitta

   A spiritual friend or someone who brings the shining merit to the people of the world and help others to attain the highest goal of life.

5. Law of Kamma

   Law of cause and effect. *Kamma* is an action or cause which is created or recreated by habitual impulse, volitions or natural energies. In popular usage, it often includes the sense of the result or effect of the action, although the proper term for this is *vipaka*. In Sanskrit, it is known as '*karma*'.

6. Nibbana

   The Pali word *Nibbana* is formed of *Ni* and *Vana*. *Ni* is a negative particle and *Vana* means lusting or craving. Known as the ultimate goal of Buddhism, it means nonattachment and may also be defined as the extinction of lust, hatred and ignorance.

7. Perfections

    These are supreme virtues to be performed by one who wishes to attain enlightenment otherwise known as '*parami*'.

8. Samma Arahang

    A mantra recited during the meditation process.

9. Samsara

    Cycle of reincarnation or rebirth in life.

10. Sotapanna

    Also known as the stream-enterer, the *sotapanna* is a partially-enlightened person, who has eradicated the first three fetters of the mind, that prevent freedom. Sotapannaship is the first of the four stages of enlightenment.

11. The Eight Worldly Conditions

Known as *Lokadhamma*, these are conditions which state that 'nothing is constant and everything is subjected to change'.

12. The Five Precepts

Codes of moral conduct in Buddhism.

13. The Right View

The right understanding of the Truth in Buddhism.

14. The Triple Gem

Known as *tiratana*, Buddhists seek refuge in the Three Gems: the Buddha, the *Dhamma* and the *Sangha*. A Buddhist relies on the Triple Gem in order to receive guidance and protection in life.

Meditation for the Attainment of Universal Love

Start by sitting in a cross-legged position, placing your right leg over the left leg. Then, place both hands on your lap, with the right hand over the left hand and the right index finger touching the left thumb. Keep your head and body erect. If you feel uncomfortable in this 'half-lotus' position, you may sit on a chair or a sofa. Adjust your sitting position until you feel that your breath and circulation can flow smoothly. Softly close your eyes and relax as if you are going to fall asleep.

Take deep breaths for a couple of times. When you breathe in, envision that you are filling every single cell in your body with renewed vigour and freshness, while allowing the air to reach the deepest part of your abdomen. When you breathe out, imagine that you are releasing all worries and anxieties from your mind. Let your mind settle down by letting go of everything, then return to breathe normally.

After relaxing your mind, you can proceed to fully relax your physical body. Relax every muscle, starting from the top of your head to the tips of your toes. The whole body should be relaxed, having no tension, contractions or stress. Up to this point, you would sense the spaciousness and comfort all over. Keep your mind cheerful, clear, pure, clean, radiant and free from thoughts. Imagine that you are sitting alone in an open space full of peace and freedom. Then, imagine that your body is hollow and empty with no organs. This would make you feel that your body is lighter and will dissolve to become one with the surrounding atmosphere.

Gently focus your mind at the centre of the body, within your abdomen at approximately two fingers' width above the navel. You should not worry about finding the exact point. Simply maintain the concentration loosely and lightly within, and never forget to relax both body and mind.

When both your body and mind are completely relaxed, you can now start to visualise an object of meditation. Visualise a round and bright midday sun that is emanating a cool radiance and has a soothing sight like the full moon. Picture the sun in your mind at ease. Do not force yourself too hard until you feel stressed. It is common if the visualised image is unclear. Try your best and maintain a peaceful, still and serene mind. If you happen to think of something else, you may recite a mantra continuously. Recite the mantra in your mind gently, allowing the mantra to slowly echo from the middle of the bright sun within your abdomen. Recite the mantra '*Samma Arahang*' repeatedly, which means 'to purify the mind in order to free oneself from all sufferings'. If this mantra sounds too foreign, you may recite the words 'clear and bright' instead. Repeat the mantra over and over whilst visualising a bright sun within until your mind comes to a standstill. Over time, your mind would leave the mantra automatically, leaving only the

The Seven Bases of the Mind

Two fingers
width above
navel

Base (1) Nostril { Left nostril for women
Right nostril for men

Base (2) Bridge of nose { Left for women
Right for men

Base (3) Middle part of head
Base (4) Roof of mouth
Base (5) Throat
Base (6) Navel
Base (7) Centre of gravity

The Seven Bases of the Mind

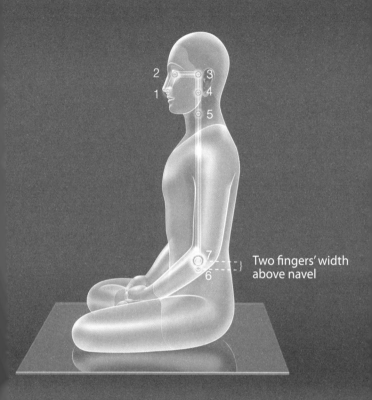

Two fingers' width above navel

Base (1) Nostril { Left nostril for women
                   Right nostril for men

Base (2) Bridge of nose { Left for women
                          Right for men

Base (3) Middle part of head
Base (4) Roof of mouth
Base (5) Throat
Base (6) Navel
Base (7) Centre of gravity

clear visualised image of the sun at the centre of your body. Be mindful of the still image that you see appearing subtly inside of you.

If there happens to be any other meditation experience in addition to your visualisation, do not be too excited or interested. Keep your mind neutral and observe whatever happens in a calm manner. Eventually, your mind will be perfectly still, settling firmly at the centre of the body. Your mind will be drawn deep within, like falling deeper into an air pocket. You will be drawn into a state where you literally fall in love with yourself in a way that you have never experienced before. Falling in love with others could bring about problems and worries, but falling in love with yourself would bring about only happiness. Soon, the *Dhamma* sphere will arise altogether with goodness in your heart.

You will attain great happiness. Brightness and joy will emerge to cleanse and purify your body, speech and mind infinitely.

Take time to share your loving kindness with others and share this pure universal love to other human beings. Start from stilling your mind at the centre and generate the feeling of loving kindness and goodwill towards everyone on Earth. Let the good feelings become one as a single and bright sun full of energy. Then, feel the bright sun which is the source of love and goodness expanding itself in all directions – to the left, right, front, back, above and below. This expanding sun represents our minds that desire all other beings to be free from suffering and attain ultimate happiness. Wish for them to discover the best thing in their lives, which is to attain the ultimate love within themselves, just like you did.

Allow your mind to expand vastly in all directions – covering yourself, the surrounding people and the location which extends as far as the horizon – till you feel that your heart has no boundaries. Let your heart extend love and goodwill to other fellow beings everywhere and in every continent of this world. This is the universal love that you should share equally to all regardless of race, faith and nationality.

About the Author

Luang Phaw Dhammajayo

Luang Phaw Dhammajayo (The Most Venerable Dhammajayo Bhikkhu) was born in Singburi Province, Central Thailand, on April 22, 1944. His interest in Buddhism began in his childhood, when he embarked in Dhamma study and continuous meditation practice, and especially when he met The Master Nun Chand Khonnokyoong (Khun Yay Ajahn). The Master Nun was an advanced Dhammakaya Meditation practitioner and instructor who was one of the forefront disciples of The Great Master Phramongkolthepmuni (Luang Pu Wat Paknam), the past famous abbot of Wat Paknam Bhasicharoen who discovered the Dhammakaya Meditation technique. She taught Luang Phaw Dhammajayo all that she knew about the Dhammakaya Meditation that she had learned from The Great Master.

When Luang Phaw Dhammajayo later graduated from Kasetsart University in Bangkok, he was ordained to the order of Buddhist monks at Wat Paknam Bhasicharoen in 1969 by his preceptor, His Holiness Somdet Phra Maharatchamongkhalachan, the present abbot of Wat Paknam Bhasicharoen. Upon his ordination into the Sangha order, he was given the name 'Dhammajayo' which means 'The Victory through Dhamma'.

In the following years, The Master Nun and Luang Phaw Dhammajayo, along with their close devotees, established a new site for meditation practice in the Khlong Sam sub-district in the Khlong Luang district of Pathum Thani province, Thailand, which has been developed into the beautiful and clean Wat Phra Dhammakaya where thousands of monks, novice monks and laymen reside. There are also tens of thousands of people who join the Buddhist ceremonies and meditation practice at the temple on a regular basis.

Since he became a Buddhist monk, Luang Phaw Dhammajayo has dedicated himself to meditation practice and instructions, Dhamma study, and the promotion of world peace through inner peace, especially for the attainment of the Dhammakaya – which he has said is the true nature that everyone can attain within, regardless of race, religion, gender, age and belief.

Presently, Luang Phaw Dhammajayo is the abbot of Wat Phra Dhammakaya and president of the Dhammakaya Foundation, which has many branches in Thailand and abroad. The foundation is very active in promoting peace, meditation practice, Dhamma study and in providing assistance to society. In addition, he also hosts the 'Inner Dreams Kindergarten Programme' through DMC which is broadcasted daily worldwide via satellites and the internet (www.dmc. tv/en). The programme is rich in Buddhist philosophy and is aimed at providing knowledge and an understanding of the truth about life concerning all beings in a modern and interesting context. The programme also provides meditation guidance and enjoyment for viewers.

Dhammakaya Meditation Societies Worldwide

Wat Phra Dhammakaya

23/2 Mu 7, Khlong Sam, Khlong Luang
Pathum Thani 12120, Thailand
Tel: +(66-2) 831-1000
       +(66-2) 524-0257 to 63
Fax: +(66-2) 524-0270 to 1
Email: info@dhammakaya.or.th
www.dhammakaya.or.th
www.meditationthai.org
www.dmc.tv/en

ASIA

BRUNEI
Co-ordination Office
Contact: Ruangrassame Chareonying
Tel: +(673) 8-867-029
Email: JY_dhamma@yahoo.com
Thailand Co-ordinator contact:
Ms. Rawiwon Mechang
Tel: +(66)-5-071-0190

CHINA
Sichuan
Sichuan Meditation Center
Tel: +(86) 28-8541-8878
+(86) 28-8129-2072
Mobile: +(86) 136-8900-7101
Email: nui072@hotmail.com
pp072@yahoo.com

HONG KONG
The Dhammakaya International Society of Hong Kong Ltd.
385-391, 2/F, Henning House, Hennessy Rd,
Wanchai, Hong Kong
Tel: +(852) 2762-7942
+(852) 2794-7485
Fax:+(852) 2573-2800
Email: dmchk@netvigator.com

JAPAN
Ibaraki
Wat Bhavana Ibaraki
2816-2 Oaza Arakawahongo, Ami-Machi,
Inashiki-gun, Ibaraki-ken, Japan 300-1152
Tel: +(81) 2-9846-6110
Mobile: +(81) 080-5489-5669
+(81) 080-5489-6659
Email: Ibaraki_otera@msn.com

Kanagawa
Wat Bhavana Kanagawa
243-4006 Kanagawaken, Ebinashi,
Kokubukita, 3-39-9, Japan
Tel: +(81) 046-205-6713
Mobile: +(81) 080-5099-4527
+(81) 080-3458-6028
Fax: +(81) 046-205-6714
Email: puwanat072@hotmail.com

Nagano
Wat Thai Nagano
733-3 Mihari, Tomi-Shi, Nagano-Ken,
389-0501, Japan
Tel: +(81) 2-6864-7516
+(81) 2-6864-7720
Fax: +(81) 2-6862-2505
Mobile: +(81) 90-9390-6055
Email: yanakuno@yahoo.com

Osaka
Wat Bhavana Osaka
Dhammakaya International Meditation Center
of Osaka
(DIMC of Osaka)
4-6-27 Ohmiya, Asahi-ku, Osaka,
535-0002, Japan
Tel: +(81) 6-6956-1400
Fax: +(81) 6-6956-1401
Email: dimcosaka@hotmail.com

Tochigi
Wat Bhavana Tochigi
1068 Oya-Machi, Utsunomiya-shi,
Tochigi-ken, Japan 321-0345
Tel: +(81) 2-8652-8701 to 2
+(81) 2-8652-8703
Email: krubajane39@hotmail.com

Tokyo
Dhammakaya International Meditation Center of Tokyo
3-78-5 Arakawa, Arakawa-ku, Tokyo,
116-0002, Japan
Tel: +(81) 3-5604-3021
Fax: +(81) 3-5604-3022
Email: chalapinyo@yahoo.com

MALAYSIA
Kuala Lumpur
Persatuan Meditasi Dhammakaya Selangor
(Dhammakaya Meditation Association,
Selangor)
4-2, Jalan Puteri 5/1, Bandar Puteri,
47100 Puchong, Selangor D.E., Malaysia
Tel: +(60) 3-8063-1882
Mobile: +(60) 17-331-1599
Email: chutintharo072@hotmail.com

Penang
Dhammakaya Meditation Center of Penang
66, Lengkonk Kenari1, Sungai Ara,
11900 Penang, Malaysia
Tel: +(60) 4-644-1854
Fax: +(60) 19-457-4270 to 1
Email: dmcpn@hotmail.com

SINGAPORE
Kalyanamitta Centre (Singapore)
30 Mohamed Sultan Road
#03-03 Lam Ann Building, Singapore 238974
Tel: +(65) 6836-1620
Email: dimcsg@dhammakaya.or.th
dimcsg@singnet.com.sg

SOUTH KOREA
Wat Tae Jong Sa
M 29-4, Dongsam-2 dong, Youndo-Gu,
Busan City, Republic of Korea
Tel:+(82) 51-405-2626
Mobile: +(82) 10-8681-5976
+(82) 10-2996-9072

TAIWAN R.O.C.
Taipei
Dhammakaya International Meditation Center of Taipei
3F No.9 Lane 16, Sec.2 Sihchuan Rd.,
Banciao city, Taipei country 220
Tel: +(886) 2-8966-1000
Fax: +(886) 2-8967-2800
http://dhammakaya.tc

Taizhong
Dhammakaya International Meditation Center of Taizhong
1-2F, No. 25, Lane 14, Minquan Rd.,
Zhong Dis, Taizhong City
Tel: +(886) 4-2223-7663

Taoyuan
Dhammakaya International Meditation
Center of Taoyuan
No. 232, Ching-Tian Street, Taoyuan City 330
Tel: +(886) 3-377-1261
Mobile: +(886) 9-2252-1072
Email: watthaitaoyuan@hotmail.com

The Middle East

BAHRAIN
DMC Centre, Bahrain
1310 Road No. 5641, Block No.0356,
Manama City, Bahrain
Contact:
Mr. Thanachai & Mrs. Peanjai Thongthae
Tel: +(973) 3960-7936
Email: s4p04u@hotmail.com

IRAN
Co-ordination Office
Contact: Ms. Aroona Puenebue
Tel: +(98) 21-2260-2105
Email: marissa_ange@yahoo.com

OMAN
Co-ordination Office
Contact: Ms. Rathanavadee Boonprasert
Tel: +(968) 9901-4584

QATAR
Co-ordination Office
Contact: Ms. Naviya Tonboonrithi
Tel: +(974) 572-7178
Email: naviyatonboonrithi@yahoo.com

SAUDI ARABIA
Co-ordination Office
Contact: Mr. Udom Chimnuan
Tel: +(966) 50-899-1912
Email: saudom_80@yahoo.com

DUBAI
Co-ordination Office
P.O.Box 33084, Dubai, UAE.
Contact:
Ms. Sangmanee Tel: +(971) 50-770-4508
Mr. Methin Tel: +(971) 50-754-0825
Ms. Dussadee Tel: +(971) 50-228-5077

The Middle East
Thailand Co-ordinator
Contact: Ms. Rawiwon Mechang
Tel: +(668)-5-071-0190
Email: rawi0072@yahoo.com

Africa

SOUTH AFRICA
Cape Town
Cape Town Meditation Centre (CMC.)
4B Homlfirth Road, Sea Point, Cape Town,
South Africa, 8005
Tel: +(27) 21-439-1896
Mobile: +(27) 72-323-0060
+(27) 79-379-0245

Johannesburg
Johannesburg Meditation Centre
30 Scheepers Street, North Riding,
Randburg, Johannesburg, South Africa 2169
Tel: +(27) 11-704-3360
Mobile: +(27) 72-363-1226
+(27) 78-464-8871
Email: info@watthaiafrica.org
somsaknow@gmail.com

Europe

BELGIUM
Antwerp
Dhammakaya International Meditation Centre (Belgium)
Sint-Jobsteenweg 84, 2970 'S-Gravenwezel,
Antwerp, Belgium
Tel: +(32) 3.326.45.77,
+(32) 3.289.51.81
Mobile: +(32) 494.32.60.02
Email: ppujakaro@hotmail.com

DENMARK
Copenhagen
Wat Buddha Denmark
Gl.Landevej 12,7130 Juelsminde, Denmark
Tel: +(45) 46.59.00.72
Mobile: +(45) 20.70.74.59
Email: dimc_dk@yahoo.com

FRANCE
Bordeaux
Wat Bouddha Bordeaux
47, Cours du General de Gaulle,
33170 Gradignan, France
Tel: +(33) 5.40.00.93.70
Mobile: +(33) 6.20.23.53.08
Email: wat_bdx@hotmail.com

Paris
Wat Bouddha Paris
10, Avenue de Paris, 77164 Ferrieres en Brie,
France
Tel: +(33) 1.64.77.28.37
Fax: +(33) 6.88.25.82.06
Email: vichak@yahoo.com

Strasbourg
Dhammakaya Centre International de la Meditation
21, Boulevard de Nancy, 67000 Strasbourg,
France
Tel: +(33) 3.88.32.69.15
Fax: +(33) 3.88.22.99.19
Email: dimcfr@yahoo.com

GERMANY
Koenigsbrunn
Dhammakaya International Meditation Zentrum (DIMZ)
Heinkel Str. 1,86343 Koenigsbrunn, Germany
Tel: +(49) 8231.957.4530
Fax: +(49) 8231.957.4532
Mobile: +(49) 162.421.0410
Email: ppadec@hotmail.com

Lovely Love

Frankfurt
Wat Buddha Frankfurt
(Meditation Verein Frankfurt Me. V)
Odenwald Str.22, 65479, Ruanheim,
Germany
Tel: +(49) 614.2833.0888
Fax: +(49) 614.2833.0890
Email: lpjon2499@hotmail.com

Stuttgart
Wat Buddha Stuttgart
Im Meissel Str.6, 71111, Waldenbuch,
Germany
Tel: +(49) 715.753.8187
Fax: +(49) 715.753.7677
Mobile: +(49) 16.0179.3782
Email: wat_stuttgart@hotmail.com

Bodensee
Wat Buddha Bodensee
Lindauer Str. 76, 88085 Langenargen,
Germany
Tel: +(49) 754.393.9777
Email: Wat_Bodensee@hotmail.com

ITALY
Milan
Wat Buddha Milano
Via Dello Scoiattolo 7 21052
Busto Arsizio (VA) Italy
Tel: +(39) 33.138.6721
+(39) 33.131.8738
Email: fortunebigbank@msn.com,
janda.a@hotmail.it

NORWAY
Midnattsol
Wat Buddha Midnattsol
(Det Norske Dhammakaya Samfunn)
Hvittingfossveien 343,
3080 Holmestrand Norway
Tel: +(47) 33.61.01.43
Mobile: +(47) 997.23.075
Fax: +(47) 33.09.66.09
Email: dhammakaya-norway@hotmail.com
http://www.dhammakaya.no

SWEDEN
Hisings Backa
Wat Buddha Gothenburg
Ostra Arodsgatan 17B, 422 43,
Hisings Backa, Sweden
Tel: +(46) -31.58.57.99
Mobile: +(46) -737.562.722
Fax: +(46) 8668-8993
Email: pworalert@hotmail.com

SWITZERLAND
Geneva
Wat Buddha Geneva, Switzerland
Avenue d'aire 93 G, 1203 Geneva, Switzerland
(c/o Wee Khee Wee)
Tel: +(41) 796.049.704
Mobile: +(33) 06.15.41.70.14

THE UNITED KINGDOM
Bristol
Wat Buddha Bristol
7 Grange Close, Bradley Stoke,
Bristol, BS32 OAH, United Kingdom
Tel: +(44) 1454-617434
Mobile: +(44) 7723-351254
Email: virandharo@hotmail.com

London
Wat Phra Dhammakaya London
(Dhammakaya International Society of
United Kingdom)
2 Brushfield Way, Knaphill, Woking,
GU21 2TG, UK
Tel: +(44) 1483-475757
+(44) 1483-480001
Fax: +(44) 1483-476161
Email: disuk@hotmail.co.uk

Manchester
Wat Charoenbhavana Manchester
Gardner House, Cheltenham Street, Salford,
Manchester M6 6WY, United Kingdom
Tel: +(44) 161-736--1633
+(44) 798-882-3616
Fax: +(44) 161-736--5747
Email: watmanchester@hotmail.com

North America

U.S.A.
California
Dhammakaya International Meditation Center (USA)
801 E. Foothill Blvd., Azusa, CA 91702 USA
Tel: +(1)-626-334-2160
Fax: +(1)-626-334-0702
Email: dimcazusa@yahoo.com
http://www.dimc.net

Florida
Florida Meditation Center
1303 N. Gordon St., Plant City,
FL 33563 USA
Tel: +(1)-813-719-8000
+(1)-813-719-8005
Fax: +(1)-813-719-8007
Email: pamotito@msn.com

Georgia
Georgia Meditation Center Inc.
4522 Tilly Mill Road, Atlanta,
GA 30360 USA
Tel: +(1)-770-452-1111
+(1)-770-643-1233
Mobile: +(1)-404-514-7721
+(1)-404-862-7559
Fax: (1)-770-452-3424
Email: somboonusa@yahoo.com

Hawaii
Hawaii Meditation Center
54-111 Maakua Rd., Hauula,
HI 97617 USA
Tel: +(1)-808-497-4072
Email: saiwa072@hotmail.com

Illinois
Meditation Center of Chicago (M.C.C.)
6224 W.Gunnison St., Chicago,
IL 60630 USA
Tel: +(1)-773-763-8763
Fax: +(1)-773-763-7897
Email: mcc_072@yahoo.com

Minnesota
Minnesota Meditation Center
242 Northdale Blvd NW, Coon Rapids,
MN 55448 USA
Tel: +(1)-763-862-6122
Fax: +(1)-763-862-6123
Email: MMC_072@yahoo.com
psuriya@hotmail.com

New Jersey
Dhammakaya International Meditation Center of New Jersey
257 Midway Ave., Fanwood,
NJ 07023 USA
Tel: +(1)-908-322-4187
+(1)-908-322-4032
Fax: +(1)-908-322-1397
Email: dimc_nj@yahoo.com

Oregon
Oregon Meditation Center
13208 SE. Stark Street., Portland,
OR 97233 USA
Tel: +(1)-503-252-3637
Mobile:+(1)-503-799-8547
Email: omc072@yahoo.com
http://www.dimcor.org

Texas
Meditation Center of Texas
1011 Thannisch Dr., Arlington,
TX 76011 USA
Tel: +(1)-817-275-7700
Email: meditation.ct.tx@gmail.com

Washington
Seattle Meditation Center
852 N.E. 83rd Street Seattle, WA 98115 USA
Tel: +(1)-206-522-1514
Fax: +(1)-206-985-2920
Email: pmsamma@hotmail.com
phracheep@yahoo.com

Virginia
Meditation Center of D.C.
3325 Franconia Rd., Alexandria,
VA 22310 USA
Tel: +(1)-703-329-0350
Fax:+(1)-703-329-0062
Email: mdc072@yahoo.com

CANADA

Ottawa

Co-ordination Office
354 Breckenridge Cres.Ottawa,
Ontario K2W1J4, Canada
Contact: Pattrawan Sukantha
Tel: 613-254-9809
613-261-4341
Email: jayy.dee@hotmail.com

Montreal

Co-ordination Office
3431 Jeanne-Manae Suite #8,
Quebec H2x2J7, Canada
Contact: Gritsana Sujjinanont
Tel: 514-845-5002
514-726-1639
Email: gritsana@netzero.net

Toronto

Contact: Pipat Sripimolphan
Tel: 647-886-0347
Email: psripimolphan@yahoo.com

Oceania

AUSTRALIA
Sydney Retreat
Wat Phra Dhammakaya, Sydney
Lot 3, Inspiration Place, Berrilee, NSW 2159
Tel: +(61) 2-9655-1128
Fax: +(61) 2-9655-1129
Mobile: +(61) 4-1162-8677
Email: Satit@dhammakaya.org.au

Sydney Office
Sydney Meditation Centre
117 Homebush Rd. Strathfield NSW 2135,
Australia
Tel: +(61) 2-9742-3031
Fax: +(61) 2-9742-3431
Mobile: +(61) 4-1145-3946
http://www.dhammakaya.org.au
http://www.dmctv.net.au

Brisbane
Brisbane Meditation Centre
73 Lodge Rd., Wooloowin, Brisbane,
QLD 4030, Australia
Tel: +(61) 7-3857-3431
Mobile: +(61) 4-3105-7215
Email: kentibkaeo@yahoo.com

Melbourne
Dhammakaya Meditation Centre of Melbourne
84 Oakwood Rd., St. Albans VIC 3021,
Australia
Tel: +(61) 3-9266-0181
Mobile: +(61) 4-0100-8799
Email: ronrawee@yahoo.com.au

Perth
Dhammakaya Meditation Centre of Perth
174 Moolanda Boulevard, Kingsley,
WA, 6026, Australia
Tel: +(61) 8-9409-8614
Fax: +(61) 8-9408-1007
Mobile: +(61) 4-302-07877
Email: phra_tawee@yahoo.com.au

Northern Beach
Northern Beach Meditation Centre
4 Hurdis Avenue, Frenchs Forest,
Sydney, Australia
Tel: +(61) 294511-722

Lovely Love

NEW ZEALAND
Orewa
Orewa Meditation Centre
43 Albatross Road, Red Beach, HBC,
Auckland, New Zealand, 1461
Tel: +(64) 9-427-4263
Fax: +(64) 9-427-4264
Mobile: +(64) 21-153-8592
Email: orewameditation@yahoo.com.au

Dunedin
Dunedin Meditation Centre (DDMC)
10 Barnes Drive, Caversham, Dunedin,
New Zealand, 9001
Tel: +(64) 3-487-6772
Fax: +(64) 3-487-6775
Email: thep072@yahoo.com

SOLOMON ISLANDS
Co-ordination Office
KITANO WKK JV P.O.BOX 1108
Honiara Solomon Islands
Contact: Mr. Sangwian Khanchaiyaphum
Tel: +(677) 24808
Fax: +(677) 25460
Email: peleyo3@hotmail.com

Credits

Honorary Consultant:
Phrabhavanaviriyakhun
(Most Ven. Dattajeevo Bhikkhu)

Consultants:
Ven. Somchai Thanavuddho (Ph.D)
Ven. Paladsudham Sudhammo
Ven. Bundit Varapanyo
Ven. Wissanu Panyateepo
Ven. Amnuaysak Munisakko
Ven. Sathien Suwannathito
Vanna Chirakiti
Metta Suvachitvong
Amporn Gibbs
Apichart Chivatxaranukul
Virongrong Ratanachaya
Winet Watthanapong

Translators:
The Dhammakaya Translation Centre
Busawan Kachonnarongvanish
Dusadee Corhiran
Jarin Kamphonphanitwong.
Nithivadee Tantipoj
Panadda Thanasuansan
Pitchayapa Siridetkoon
Pittaya Wong
Shinavit Sukhawat
Suchada Thongmalai
Supichaya Panprasert
Suganda Cluver

Rewriter:
Sarinee Vorasubin

Executive Editors:
Ven. Sanchaya Nakajayo
Wichaya Triwichien
Walailuck Mongkolkawil
Pittaya Wong

Editor-in-Chief:
Wichaya Triwichien

Editors:
Chanida Jantrasrisalai (Ph.D)
Jennifer Kitil
Marc Hubbard
Sarinee Vorasubin
Supakij Nantarojanaporn
Surin Chaturaphit

Editorial Staffs:
Boriboon Noreevej
Karawee Chokkunawadtana
Lalintip Suwanmaneedang
Methinee Tangrapeepakorn
Nirada Vaisayanunt
Prawee Thamarak
Soodpradtana Jaruchart

Design & Art Direction:
Metta Suvachitvong
DM&S Advertising Co., Ltd.
The Print Lodge Pte. Ltd.

The Publisher would also like to extend appreciation
to all individuals who have contributed in one way
or another towards the success of this book.

Contributors

Distinguished Contributors

Anant Asavabhokhin

Boonchai Bencharongkul

Prakob Chirakiti (Ph.D)

Vanna Chirakiti

Sakol - Song Watcharasriroj

Metta Suvachitvong

Apichart Chivatxaranukul

Honorary Contributors

Ven. Somchai Thanavuddho (Ph.D)
Bhanapot - Busaba - Bolaphum Damapong
Sivaya Soranapipat
Supasith-Manothip-Nattarapat Jakawaldham
Supawadee Dokin, Kawin Hokken

Sponsoring Contributors

Wat Charoenbhavana Manchester
Ven. Pratchaya Sotthijanyo
& supporters of Wat Bhavana D.C.
Wanwisa Ubolsuwan

Supporting Contributors

Wat Bhavana Ibaraki
Wat Bhavana Kanagawa
Wat Bhavana Osaka
Wat Bhavana Tochigi
Wat Bouddha Bordeaux
Wat Bouddha Paris
Wat Buddha Bodensee
Wat Buddha Bristol
Wat Buddha Denmark
Wat Buddha Frankfurt

Wat Buddha Gothenburg
Wat Buddha Midnattsol
Wat Buddha Milano
Wat Buddha Stuttgart
Wat Tae Jong Sa
Wat Thai Nagano
Brisbane Meditation Centre
DMC Centre, Bahrain
Florida Meditaion Center
Hawaii Meditation Center

Meditation Center of D.C.   Orewa Meditation Centre
Meditation Center of Texas   Seattle Meditation Center
Oregon Meditation Center   Sichuan Meditation Center
Dhammakaya Centre International De La Meditation
Dhammakaya International Meditation Center (USA)
Dhammakaya International Meditation Center of Indonesia
Dhammakaya International Meditation Center of New Jersey
Dhammakaya International Meditation Center of Taipei
Dhammakaya International Meditation Center of Taizhong
Dhammakaya International Meditation Center of Taoyuan
Dhammakaya International Meditation Center of Tokyo
Dhammakaya International Meditation Centre (Belgium)
Dhammakaya International Meditation Zentrum (DIMZ)
The Dhammakaya International Society of Hong Kong Ltd.
Dhammakaya Meditation Center of Kuala Lumpur
Dhammakaya Meditation Center of Penang
Dhammakaya Meditation Centre of Melbourne
Dhammakaya Meditation Centre of Perth
Cape Town Meditation Centre (CMC)
Dunedin Meditation Centre (DDMC)
Wat Buddha Geneva, Switzerland
Wat Phra Dhammakaya London
Wat Phra Dhammakaya, Sydney
Georgia Meditation Center Inc.
Johannesburg Meditation Centre
Kalyanamitta Centre (Singapore)
Meditation Center of Chicago (MCC)
Minnesota Meditation Center
Northern Beach Meditation Centre

Co-Ordination Office of Brunei
Co-Ordination Office of Dubai
Co-Ordination Office of Iran
Co-Ordination Office of Montreal
Co-Ordination Office of Oman
Co-Ordination Office of Ottawa
Co-Ordination Office of Qatar
Co-Ordination Office of Saudi Arabia
Co-Ordination Office of Solomon Islands

Ven.Chaifa Dhanyakulo
Ven.Chanwit Warawitcho
Ven.Chatpong Katapunno
Ven.Chayut Thanutamo
Ven.Karun Karunyako
Ven.Monchai Aphichano
Ven.Narong Dantacitto
Ven.Panake Thanasakko
Ven.Poolsak Punnasakko
Ven.Santi Jittasanto

Ven.Songwut Chayawuttho
Ven.Teerapat Yanapattho
Ven.Udom Yatissaro
Ven.Uttaphon Punyanato
Ven.Vichit Siripunno
Ven.Wanchai Katanatho
Ven.Wicha Adhivijo
Ven.Wut Suvuddhiko
Bhikkhu # 16 "Pathomsompoch"
Rev.Piyanat Preampramot

Anongnuch Choungrangsee
Anupong Hochitsiriyanont
Atsadang Sridee
Booncharutwong Family
Busaracam-Nara Sarikabut
Chalinee Anthawornphong
Issaree Thaninkitiwong

Jessica Lim
Jirapatr Chuaratanaphong
Kaltongpan Saejia
Keyoon Wilawan & Family
Kittichai Chuaratanaphong
Kururat Group
Malee Gantuptim

Lovely Love

Nathawan Viseskul

Panthong Fugitt

Parnto Family

Phantipha Koomphet

Pissamai Sanghirun

Puttaraksa Group.

Ratana Katephasook

Reception Division (MDR)

Ruangvit Thanasothorn

Ruchta Kaumchoen

Sang Arayasakdakul

Santi-Pimjai Tissayakorn

Sirin Tiyanon

Sirinart Buttaratha

Siripak Tundomrongpong

Sirivasaeree Family

Siwalai Thanapatra

Somchai Anantaphruti

Sopit-Thitima Kongsri

Sudarat Tantitrakanwattana

Suleeporn Sujarat

Supachai Srisupaaksorn

Sureenart Chuaratanaphong

Surisa Pamtim

Sysmll L.Warfield

Teerapatr Chuaratanaphong

Uriwan Pasook & Family

Verasak-Areerat Sirikururat

Verasuita Chuaratanaphong

Vincent Black

Wipas Raksakulthai

www.beautyhealth.tht.m

Chettabudr Waraporn & Families

Dhatsamrej Group (The Winning Mind)

Dr.Mongkol Sae-Chua & Family

Dr.Pranod-Tasneya Pipatanangkura

Dr.Sunchai-Maleewan Leethochawalit

Enomoto Kouichi-Priyada-Kimoe

Kawee-Sukanya Wetchayanwiwat

Pornthep Dechasilapachaikul

Pronpen-Nittaya Toosiripattana

Sachon Prasertying, Sathita Serirodom

Sangoun-Pattra-Yaowanee Srisataporn

Chotimon Adul-Yaowapa-Arpapan-Noppadol

Sujinda-Nicolas-Parin-Lillada Chaipanich
Suwan Chaikittipornlert & Family
Suwanna Saetang & Tantiniramai Family
Naruemon Jintapatthanakit, Jeerasak Meesuksabai
Natsuang Wongwatunyu, Fundul Lohanut
Guydow Boonyarattaphan-Weerawat Suwannapirom
Jindarat-Takaaki Sasagawa & Tokyo Business Forum
Jittrong-Prancc-Nuttawat-Soodpradtana Jaruchart
Phakmanee Family & Duangkeaw Dormitory
Niklas-Wiola-Sivaporn Lonnerfors, Atitaya Piputkamalaket
Chompoonuch-Kamolchanok-Saichon-Tharadol Rodthanom

The Publisher would like to rejoice in the merit of all
contributors, as well as those whose names may not be
presented in this book.

Tomorrow The World Will Change

Luang Phaw Dhammajayo

"The dream of world peace will never come true if the dreamer is unable to find his or her own inner contentment. Once everyone experience inner happiness, true world peace will occur."

What would a world of peace be like?

In the light of never-ending conflicts, wars and terrorist threats, peace is something that seems unattainable. Constantly wrought with uncertainty and hostility, life on this planet sometimes does seem lacklustre and lacking in joy; much less peaceful.

While most of us would think that the dream of world peace coming true is akin to catching the wind with our bare hands, Luang Phaw Dhammajayo, abbot of Dhammakaya Temple and president of Dhammakaya Foundation, brings an encouraging message: that world peace is within reach ... and all it takes is a simple practice.

Through the act of meditation – stilling the mind and focusing the mind at the centre of the body – every individual, regardless of race, culture and religion, can experience inner happiness that will ultimately perpetuate goodness and harmony on earth. Innate happiness, through meditation, has the power to purge inner demons such as greed and anger – the root cause of strife on earth – from the hearts of humanity.

Discover how you, as an individual, can gain a deeper understanding of life to combat the negativities of this world by first reaching an inner calm. *Tomorrow The World Will Change* not only gives you an overview on how meditation can make you a better person; it teaches you how to master meditation through its step-by-step meditation guide.

ISBN: 978-981-05-7757-5 (Singapore)
96 pages • 105mm (W) x 170mm (H)

Journey to Joy

Luang Phaw Dhammajayo

Life is not merely an external voyage to achieve our goals; it is a journey whereby we look into ourselves and embark on the path to self-discovery for the attainment of Dhammakaya — the true refuge within everyone.

Within the pages of this book, Luang Phaw Dhammajayo shares how meditation plays a part in enriching peoples' lives. Meditation brings about bountiful love, instils hope and willpower, develops closer family relationships, increases a person's knowledge, enhances peoples' careers and leads them to unearth their inner wisdom and their ability to create everlasting peace.

To meditate, simply close your eyes, concentrate on the stillness and rest your focus at the seventh base of your body, two fingers' width above the navel. Experience absolute serenity and bliss by relaxing your mind and body in the process.

Your future lies in your hands. The journey towards ultimate happiness begins with you. Start meditation today and witness the positive changes in your life unfold before you!

ISBN: 978-981-05-9637-8 (Singapore)
368 pages • 110mm (W) x 178mm (H)

Lovely Love

Luang Phaw Dhammajayo

Love, like all things in life, can be transient. Pure love, however, is lasting and it gives without necessarily bargaining for a return.

Within the pages of this book, Luang Phaw Dhammajayo teaches us how to love unselfishly by advocating that it does not matter whom you love, or how you love, but that you just love. A superior love that supersedes all others is universal love – a love which is pure, clean, complete and powerful. The best news is universal love can be attained simply through meditation. Meditating allows your mind to experience peace, pure happiness and pure love.

Reveal in the fact that the sole happiness in life is to love and be loved. Speak lovingly, think lovingly and act lovingly towards others and experience the infinite joy that pure love will bring into your life consequentially!

ISBN: 978-981-08-0044-4 (Singapore)
188 pages • 110mm (W) x 178mm (H)

The following book are available by mail-order:

Tomorrow The World Will Change

US$9.95

Journey to Joy

US$18.00/book
US$180.00/series [10 books]

Lovely Love

US$14.00/book
US$84.00/series [6 books]

Prices exclude postage and packing

Please send your enquiries or orders to:

The Print Lodge Pte Ltd
16 Arumugam Road
#03-04 Lion Building D
Singapore 409961
Tel: [65] 6746 6520
Fax: [65] 6746 6578
Email: matthew@theprintlodge.com.sg